*This book belongs to*

____________________

*a woman after*
*God's own Heart.*

# Following God with All Your Heart

Elizabeth George

HARVEST HOUSE PUBLISHERS
EUGENE, OREGON

Italics in Scripture verses indicate author emphasis.

*Cover photo © Thomas Dobner / Alamy; back cover author photo © Harry Langdon*

*Cover by Dugan Design Group, Bloomington, Minnesota*

**FOLLOWING GOD WITH ALL YOUR HEART**
Copyright © 2008 by Elizabeth George
Published by Harvest House Publishers
Eugene, Oregon 97402
www.harvesthousepublishers.com

Library of Congress Cataloging-in-Publication Data

George, Elizabeth.
Following God with all your heart / Elizabeth George.
p. cm.
ISBN-13: 978-0-7369-0504-6 (pbk.)
ISBN-10: 0-7369-0504-9 (pbk.)
1. Christian women—Religious life. 2. Christian life—Biblical teaching. 3. Joshua (Biblical figure) I. Title.
BV4527.G4585 2008
248.8'43—dc22

2008017250



**Printed in the United States of America**

11 12 13 14 15 16 / VP-NISK / 10 9 8 7 6 5 4

# *Contents*

# *An Invitation*

I'm often asked what prompts me to write a certain book, and you may be wondering the same thing as you hold this book in your hands. I usually point to several landmarks along my spiritual journey with God.

As a brand-new Christian at 28 years old, I was challenged to begin memorizing Scripture. I dutifully began to memorize Bible verses by carrying packets of them around to read whenever I had a spare moment. Every one of the verses I've learned by heart is precious to me, but some of them regularly come to my rescue or spur me on each time I encounter a crossroad while seeking to follow God with all my heart.

The six verses I emphasize in this book have been my particular and constant advisors for the past three decades. They've seen me through many an anxious moment and motivated me to obedience as I stared at the unknown and when everything in me wanted to balk at doing what God was asking of me simply because I'd never done it before.

As I began to grow in Christ, I learned that I, like all Christians, was saved for a purpose. I had a mission from God, so to speak. He wanted me to worship Him and serve Him.[1] I also began to realize God had a plan for my life. While this was exciting, it was also frightening. The usual scenario went like this: I had dreams... but I was afraid. I had opportunities...but I was afraid.

The six verses spotlighted in this book once again came to my rescue and continue to do so. They not only supply solid encouragement, but they give me insights into the second half of my mission—to serve God and live out His plan.

Then I encountered the issue of obedience. Following God and fulfilling His mission to serve Him wholeheartedly is sometimes a struggle. People are sinful. We are lazy. We are fearful. We are foolish. Even the apostle Paul admitted to such struggles. He wrote, "I know that nothing good dwells in me, that is, in my flesh; for the willing is present in me, but the doing of the good is not. For the good that I want, I do not do, but I practice the very evil that I do not want" (Romans 7:18-19 NIV).

Well, friend, these six precious verses have helped me stay focused in my desire to pursue God totally, without reservation—to trust Him, to step out in faith, to take the risks, to do the growing, to follow His leading, and to seek and live His plan and His will day by day. They have helped me gain victory in my quest to believe and live out God's purposes. They have given me the assurance that I can trust God and move forward toward fulfilling His plan for my life with *success, courage, strength, humility, contentment,* and *confidence.*

I'm offering you my special handful of scriptures with a heartfelt prayer that they will change your life. That they will challenge you to greater levels of spiritual growth and maturity. That they will help you move forward in your desire to become, by God's grace…

…a successful woman (Joshua 1:8)

…a courageous woman (Joshua 1:9)

…an exceptional woman (Romans 12:2)

…a humble woman (1 Peter 5:5-6)

…a contented woman (Psalm 84:11)

…a confident woman (Philippians 4:13)

And now, "my beloved [sister], be steadfast, immovable, always abounding in the work of the Lord, knowing that your toil is not in vain in the Lord" (1 Corinthians 15:58). May you…

Trust in the Lord with all your heart.

Seek Him with all your heart.

Love Him with all your heart.

Praise Him with all your heart.

Follow Him with all your heart.

Serve Him with all your heart.

And live His will with all your heart

…and live it to the hilt![2]

# Section 1

# *Becoming a Successful Woman*

*In whatever man does without God,*
*he must fail miserably*
*or succeed more miserably.*

George MacDonald

1

# *Success Made Simple*

*This Book of the Law shall not depart from your mouth,*
*but you shall meditate in it day and night,*
*that you may observe to do*
*according to all that is written in it.*
*For then you will make your way prosperous,*
*and then you will have good success.*

JOSHUA 1:8

As I begin this book about following God with all our hearts, I just came in the house after standing in the driveway waving to my daughter, Courtney, and her four little ones. They're driving to the navy base at Pearl Harbor to finalize their move to Hawaii. And, I might add, this is the third hectic day in a row they've come and gone. But no matter. We all just witnessed a double rainbow! That incredible sight and the fact that my daughter is happily following her navy husband as he serves his country and pursues his career makes me glad. Why? Because she is living what I'm writing about in this book. In her different and sometimes difficult roles of wife to a submariner and mother of four young children, Courtney is successfully following God with all her heart.

God may not be asking you to move your family to Hawaii, although that might not be so bad, but He *is* asking you to follow

Him wherever you are and whatever is facing you. How can you be successful in following God in all the roles and responsibilities He has for you? He'll show you the way...if you let Him.

## *God Shows You the Way to Success*

Will you be encouraged to know God addresses "success" in the Bible? He does! In fact, He gives us a step-by-step plan for arriving at *true* success in our endeavors and our lives. When you follow His simple guidelines laid out in Joshua 1:8 and 9, God's blessings are lavished on your efforts and perseverance:

> 8 This Book of the Law shall not depart from your mouth, but you shall meditate in it day and night, that you may observe to do according to all that is written in it. For then you will make your way prosperous, and then you will have good success.
>
> 9 Have I not commanded you? Be strong and of good courage; do not be afraid, nor be dismayed, for the Lord your God is with you wherever you go.

I first found God's plan for success as a new Christian. Even though I was 28 years old, married to my Jim for eight years, and a struggling mom of two preschool girls, I knew nothing about God's ways or His definitions of success. Almost all I had experienced was the opposite of anything related to success. I knew the taste and feel of failure.

Fortunately, by God's grace, I accepted Jesus as my God and Savior. Then, at the urging of mature Christians, I began memorizing Bible verses right away. The second verse (verses, in this case) I learned by heart was Joshua 1:8-9. I printed it out in a 3 x 5 spiral notebook, propped it up in the windowsill over my kitchen sink, and spent weeks—*weeks!*—learning it. In fact, almost a month. But oh, what a passage! Read verse 8 again. Now you see why it took me so long to memorize it. This verse is God's recipe for success.

I want us to see it, taste it, take it in, and know it. And it all begins with Joshua, a man who followed God with all his heart.

### *A Man Who Wholeheartedly Followed God*

Are you wondering why a book for women is beginning with a man, with someone named Joshua?

- Joshua desired to follow God wholeheartedly.
  *And I'm guessing you're like me and want to do that too.*
- Joshua was given huge responsibilities.
  *And you've been given your own list of jobs.*
- Joshua was a warrior for God.
  *So are you.* (The meaning of "virtuous," used to describe God's ideal woman in Proverbs 31:10, is also used to describe a warrior.)
- Joshua wanted to be successful at the jobs God gave him.
  *I imagine you do too.*

When I began memorizing Joshua 1:8, I didn't know anything about this man of God except one line of a song I'd heard as a child: "Joshua fought the battle of Jericho, and the walls came tumbling down." I wondered, *Just who is this guy anyway?* And I found out.

*Joshua was a friend and aide to Moses.* As Moses' helper, Joshua was allowed to travel halfway up Mount Sinai with Moses, God's leader of His people, and he was present when God personally issued His law to Moses. Joshua was also with Moses when God spoke to him face-to-face as with a friend. Joshua, a friend of Moses from his youth, was privy to the personal relationship Moses enjoyed with God as a man who followed Him with all his heart. Joshua saw Moses' faith, witnessed his obedience, felt his heart, observed his leadership of God's people, and received his teaching…for 40 years.

Like his mentor, Joshua followed the Lord faithfully. He also spoke with and listened to God (Joshua 1:1). That's when Joshua was given the command: "Arise, go over this Jordan." God was saying, "Go to the other side of the river. You know, to the place where the heathens and barbarians live. You know, the land of the giants. That's where My people's inheritance awaits. Yours too! And by the way, Joshua, you'll have to take it by force, through battles."

Hearing God's commands and assignments must have caused Joshua to quake in his sandals. And the Lord obviously knew of Joshua's doubts and fears because three times in the first chapter of the book of Joshua, God tells this soldier to "be strong and of good courage":

- "Be strong and of good courage, for to this people *you shall divide as an inheritance the land which I swore to their fathers to give them*" (verse 6).
- "Only be strong and very courageous, that you may observe to do according to all the law which Moses My servant commanded you; do not turn from it to the right or to the left, *that you may prosper wherever you go*" (verse 7).
- "Be strong and of good courage; do not be afraid, nor be dismayed, *for the Lord your God is with you wherever you go*" (verse 9).

Did you notice that after each command God pronounced a golden promise? (I put them in italics for you.) Be sure to take note of them! Like Joshua, on the other side of your obedience is God's blessing.

*Joshua was Moses' successor.* Why was God giving this command to Joshua? Because Moses, the great leader of the Israelites, died. God passed the leadership of His people to Joshua. What a staggering responsibility! Imagine taking on the task of motivating approximately 2.5 million obstinate, murmuring, complaining, cantankerous, rebellious people.[1] And not just govern them, but lead them into battle! Yet this was God's assignment for Joshua. As a military commander and warrior, he was to guide this difficult group into the Promised Land and take it by force.

Moses was a shepherd before he led the people. And his instrument for leading was a rod, a shepherd's tool. But Joshua? He was a warrior, and he would lead with a sword and spear. And both weapons would certainly be needed because the land across the Jordan River was filled with enemies and giant soldiers. And not one of them wanted to hand over their land to an outside people. No, they would surely fight to keep what was theirs!

And Joshua was coming behind Moses, the greatest leader the world had known up until then—maybe even *ever!* (Except Jesus, of course.) Yes, Joshua had big shoes to fill. Nothing was going to *be* easy for him. And nothing was going to *come* easily for him.

## *A Woman's Heart for God*

I'm glad I discovered early in my Christian life what led up to the life-guiding, confidence-building, success-producing words God spoke to Joshua's fearful heart in Joshua 1, verses 8 and 9. In my memory of the day I learned about this warrior, I can still see me sitting at my desk, surrounded by the research books that told me so much about this flesh-and-blood man who feared the path in front of him yet followed God's command to walk it. I sat there stunned, thinking, *Wow! This is me too. And this is so pertinent for me as a woman. God has given me great responsibilities. He's given me a huge job description as His child, as a wife, as a mom to two little girls, as the one in charge of running our household and home. And He also expects me to nurture a heart for Him, grow spiritually, and serve His people. Yes, I can definitely relate to Joshua's feelings as he received his marching orders. It's scary!*

And it's true. Christian women have demanding tasks to tackle, many of which have to be faced and taken care of every day. God also has His goals for each and every one of us. In the Bible He spells out His instructions to us regarding our roles. And then there are the character qualities He asks us to develop, along with the kind deeds, goodness, and assistance He charges us to extend to everyone. Plus we're to be ever-growing in our knowledge of Him, improving our walk with Him, employing our gifts in service, giving ministry to many, witnessing to those who don't know Christ, being ideal workers on our jobs, serving God, working to be helpful and loving daughters and daughters-in-law and family members, and...and...and...and... *Whew!* On and on our assignments go.

I'm chuckling as I recall reading and reviewing a particular book for a Christian bookstore. The writer listed what she labeled "the six biggest stressors in a woman's life":

#1 children

#2 lack of time

#3 disagreements with husbands

#4 financial problems

#5 housework, housework, housework

#6 career or job outside the home

Oh yes! I definitely related to all of these. Take #5, for instance—housework. Truly, a woman's work is *never* done, even when we think it is. One Tuesday I got my home all cleaned up. That night my two daughters, who lived in dorms at a nearby college, came home with some friends to get a little taste of home away from home. I had homemade soup on the stove, which they helped themselves to. They enjoyed a fun visit by the fire before they went back to their places.

The next morning as I turned the corner into the kitchen, there it was—a genuine mess. Soup was slopped on the stove, into the burners, down the front of the oven, and even on the floor. The group had also made cookies and left the dirty pans, mixer bowl, beaters, and measuring cups for...guess who? I guess for me. As I was cleaning up, I thought, *Didn't I just do this? It isn't even 24 hours since I did this, and my kitchen is in shambles. Housework just goes on and on.*

One book I refer to often addresses the variety of seasons that come in a marriage. It details the different challenges that accompany each age and stage, beginning with the "getting to know you" romance and all its freshness and expectations and moving through the decades of marriage, right down to the reality of preparing for death of you or your spouse.

Like Joshua, who was told to care for God's people, go into battle, face giants, defeat enemies, and conquer the land, my heart sometimes feels fearful and overwhelmed by what's here and what's to come.

Like Joshua, I need encouragement.

Like Joshua, I often wonder if I can live up to God's expectations. Can I really carry out His assignments?

And like Joshua, I need a sure formula from God to follow so I can have the confidence to remain steadfast and persistent in the things I know are right. I want to "keep on keeping on" in fulfilling my desire to be what God wants me to be and do what He wants me to do—to be a woman with a heart for Him.

### *Success Starts with Following God's Word*

Life is filled with challenges, assignments, necessities, routines, work, and surprises. And it's easy—and natural—to feel anxious, afraid, and inadequate at times...just like I do and evidently like

Joshua did. He was very young compared to Moses (who was 120 when he died and Joshua took over the leadership). Joshua was fearful as he thought about going to war against giants and other foes with his band of untrained former slaves. (The Hebrews had been Egyptian slaves for more than 400 years.) Joshua may have even been tired before he began. Perhaps he wondered like I sometimes do, *But how, Lord? How am I going to do all this? How am I going to fulfill Your commands? I want to follow You with all my heart...but how, oh how, Lord? Help me!*

*As we obediently and unwaveringly believe in and follow God's promises, His blessing and success are ours.*

I'll bet you've had these same thoughts, questions, and fears. As you stand and gaze at your to-do list from God, at the tasks He's given you, at the multitude of responsibilities that fall on your shoulders to carry and bear, at the work involved in what God expects you to handle, at increasing pain as you face physical challenges, God's Word reaches out to you with encouragement and instructions. And this was spoken first to Joshua to give him confidence as he faced a seemingly impossible situation:

> This Book of the Law shall not depart from your mouth, but you shall meditate in it day and night, that you may observe to do according to all that is written in it (Joshua 1:8).

These instructions contain a simple charge—*know God's Word and do it.* If we choose to follow God's advice, He assures us of "good success" or "prosperity" in the rest of this verse. In other words, there will be a successful outcome due to the courage, confidence, hope of victory, and wisdom that comes only from focusing fully on God's Word and His promises. As we obediently and unwaveringly believe in and follow God's promises—refusing to succumb to our fears, doubts, inabilities, and tiredness—His blessing and success are ours.

God gave Joshua directions—and hope—through these words. And the same directions and hope are yours too. It's success made simple: If you know God's Word and do God's Word, you will be successful in your endeavors, in meeting and fulfilling your job assignments from God, in pleasing Him as you move forward in confidence.

## *Moving Forward*

Where does God have you today? What roles and responsibilities have you been given? What are your dreams and desires? Many of these aspirations indicate God's direction for your life. Please take some time to find out what God's Word says about your roles and to pray about them. Why not jot down some dreams you have too? Write them down in your Bible, your prayer book, your journal, or your special notebook dedicated to dreaming and planning.

And if you don't know God's plan and purpose for your life today, and you can't point to any dreams for serving Him in the future, start today to realize the goals He has for you and make them your own. It's hard moving forward if you don't know where to head. Once you understand where you're supposed to go, know what you're supposed to do, and have goals to help you get there…

- you can start praying about them. Daily prayer fuels your forward movement toward God's special plan and purpose for *you*. (Remember, God only asked one person to lead the 2.5 million people—Joshua.)
- you can also begin finding out what God has to say about your duties and dreams. As you discover the answers in God's Word, they will give

you specific direction and greater confidence as uncertainties are removed.

- you can look for teachers, mentors, classes, and books to help you. (Even Joshua had to be taught by Moses so he would be able to fulfill God's purposes.)
- you can memorize verses that give you confidence and encourage you in your pursuit of your goals. (God told Joshua to know and meditate on His Word.)
- you can map out steps that will move you toward successfully reaching and fulfilling God's job assignments. (I'm sure the warrior, Joshua, had a battle plan!)

As you reach toward your golden goals, things will happen. Count on it! Like Joshua, obstacles and emotions are sure to loom up along your road to success. They'll stretch you, test you, and grow you. And each step taken in the power of God's Word, in spite of a multitude of challenges, moves you into a closer relationship with God. His all-powerful Word will encourage and strengthen you all along the way. Yes, you'll probably fail, fall back, foul up, and fall down more times than you'd like. But be like Joshua—relying on God, doing what He says and asks of you in His Word, and praying all the way. This will give you the desire and confidence—and power!—to keep growing. And as you faithfully follow God, you will prosper. You will enjoy God's kind of success. You will be blessed by Him.

*He who walks according to God's Word*
*acts wisely and happily,*
*but he who goes according to his own head*
*acts unwisely and to no profit.*

Martin Luther

2

# *The Starting Point for Success*

*This Book of the Law shall not depart from your mouth,*
*but you shall meditate in it day and night,*
*that you may observe to do*
*according to all that is written in it.*
*For then you will make your way prosperous,*
*and then you will have good success.*

JOSHUA 1:8

I love writing books, and I also love reading books. So I'm a regular visitor to online and brick-and-mortar bookstores...not to mention lots of airport book nooks, racks, stores, and kiosks. I can't help it! I'm astounded at how many titles promise "keys" or "steps" or "ways" or "secrets" to success. And, amazingly, they all seem to sell well. I suppose it's because we naturally desire to accomplish our goals and find and fulfill our purposes. We *want* to be successful at home and in our families. We *want* to be good on the job and excellent in our activities, hobbies, passions, and skills.

One of the greatest messages ever written on success is in the Bible, in Joshua 1:8-9. These words contain the way to sure success. Take a minute to read again the verse written at the beginning of this chapter—verse 8. As you do, remember we closed the last chapter with a challenge to think about our lives and responsibilities, about our dreams and goals, about success as seen through God's eyes.

Okay, let's look at the starting point to success and how it will spur us on as we follow God with all our hearts.

### *The Origin of Success*

Did you notice the five words that launch God's instructions for success? "This Book of the Law." The Bible is divine truth. God and His Word are the beginning of a life of blessing, the starting point for success in all that really matters. It's like this. When God and His Word dwell in your heart, occupy your thoughts, and guide your steps, He blesses your efforts and enterprises.

The Bible isn't magic. And reading it doesn't make you lucky. But it is powerful. In fact, it's dynamite! And here's why.

*The Bible is God's Word*—There's nothing like it because it comes from Him. "All Scripture is given by inspiration of God" (2 Timothy 3:16). The Bible is God-breathed. And because it springs from Him, we can completely trust it as coming to us straight from His heart to ours.

*The Bible is alive*—It's life-changing! God's Word shapes our lives, actively working in us...and on us. It's "living and powerful, and sharper than any two-edged sword, piercing even to the division of soul and spirit, and of joints and marrow, and is a discerner of the thoughts and intents of the heart" (Hebrews 4:12). Like a surgeon's knife, God's truths cut into our inner lives—our thoughts, motives, attitudes, desires, and intentions—to reveal them for what they are.

*God's Word is a map you can safely follow as you travel through life.*

*The Bible is a force*—It actively works in us and for us, "like a fire...[and] a hammer that breaks the rock in pieces" (Jeremiah 23:29).

*The Bible is a defense against temptation*—Jesus fought Satan's onslaught of temptations and lies by declaring each time He was enticed by the devil, "It is written..." and then quoting Scripture (Matthew 4). Like our Master, we do battle against Satan's attacks with "the sword of the Spirit, which is the word of God" (Ephesians 6:17). God's Word protects us as a piece of "the whole armor of God" (verse 13).

*The Bible is a guide*—Its truths lead us. Do you ever feel lost? In need of advice and direction? God's Word is a map you can safely follow as you travel through life. The psalmist admitted he was "a stranger in the earth" and begged God not to hide His commandments...His direction (Psalm 119:19). He said God's Word would lead him like "a lamp to my feet and a light to my path" (verse 105).

## *The Power of God's Word*

There's no doubt that God's Word taken to heart translates into power, wisdom, and ministry—seen and unseen. I've witnessed that transformation! For instance,

> At one time in our spiritual growth process, Jim and I had the opportunity to hear a guest speaker at our church. He was Harold Lindsell, the editor of *Christianity Today* magazine at the time. He visited our Young Marrieds Sunday school class after speaking from the pulpit during the church service. His format for our class was a question-and-answer time. One by one, and one after another, he fielded and answered any and all questions.
>
> At that time Jim was a seminary student intent on learning as much as he could about the Bible. And he was absolutely in awe of and blown away by Dr. Lindsell's deep and profound knowledge and understanding of the

Bible. Jim was so impressed by this giant of the faith that he asked him afterward, "How did you answer all those questions? How did you know all that information?"

And Dr. Lindsell's answer? Jim fully expected him to report a long line of educational experiences, time spent and degrees earned in study at a Bible college, seminary, or prestigious university. But no! Dr. Lindsell told Jim that for the past 40 years he'd been reading through his Bible once every year. He explained that he'd worked out a system that allowed him to finish his Bible reading each year on December 15, so he could enjoy extended family time at Christmas as well as ensure a few extra days if there were any scriptures he'd missed or wanted to go back over.

The knowledge of God's Word—dwelling deeply in this man's heart, mind, and soul, and pursued for decades—provided the ready answers to questions about the Bible and life issues. It also gave him the courage and confidence to powerfully speak the truth, whether in a group setting or on the pages of the prestigious *Christianity Today*.

## *The Influence of God's Word*

We've been talking about success and seeing God's Word as the starting point. As a young Christian I knew I needed help, and one special woman was there for me. In fact, she changed my life! From the first day I met her, I admired her industry and her use of time in doing things that were truly important. Her manner was patient, friendly, confident, helpful, and even businesslike as she went about the Lord's business. I watched her in public and studied how she dealt with people. I noticed how she spoke to them—her choice of words, her tone of voice. I listened any time she shared in a classroom or gathering, taking in the content of her words. She was a constant fountain of encouragement, comfort, counsel, affirmation, exhortation, and exaltation of the Lord...all out of and using God's Word as her source of wisdom and knowledge. She was a true woman of influence, using God's Word and its power to positively impact many—including me.

Finally I mustered up the nerve to ask about her devotional time. I gulped and dared to go even further and ask, "*What* do you read in the Bible? And *when* do you read it? And *where* do you read it?" I wanted specifics. I wanted to know everything in detail because I was going to do whatever she did that was so powerful. She explained that she'd divided her Bible reading in a way that enabled her to read it quarterly. Yes, that's right—four times a year. No wonder she had so much to give! It's true—"something coming in" equals "something going out." It was clear that what she was doing enabled her to be so helpful and successful in ministering to all who crossed her path.

## The Force of Reading God's Word

Can you handle another illustration on the impact of Scripture? My husband was dean of Admissions at The Master's Seminary in California for many years. One church in California sent student after student after student to the seminary. One day Jim got a call that 12 more young men from this church were interested in attending the school. Amazing! They asked if Jim would please drive to their city and meet with the group. They'd concluded that it would be easier for Jim (one person) to come to them rather than have all 12 guys come to him.

*What is going on at that church?* Jim wondered. *Why is so much fruit being produced from one congregation?* He found out. The pastor to the college-age adults had challenged his group to read 15 chapters in their Bibles *each* day. This schedule moved them through the Bible four times a year. Such concentration and exposure to God's truth created a force for wanting to know even more about the Bible. It also motivated and instructed them to let others know the power of the Scriptures so they could fall in love with God and His Word too.

## The Impact of Reading Scripture

I have a confession to make. At the time Jim met with this amazing—and absolutely committed—group of students who were following God with all their hearts, our two daughters were also in college. I was so convicted when Jim told me about the group's pastor and his assignment. My thinking about my girls and their friends had been, *How can someone ask a college student to read 15 chapters of the Bible a day? They've got their classwork, their essays, papers, and exams. And they have their jobs on top of their schoolwork. They never get enough sleep as it is, and they're always behind in their studies.*

Okay, I admit I was babying my girls. They were getting the kid glove treatment from their mom. At the most, I encouraged them to be faithful to spend *some* time with God each day, *some* time in His Word, *some* time in prayer. But time for 15 chapters a day? Yet this college group had leaped on their pastor's suggestion, and they were flooding out of that church in all directions with a burning desire to serve God and share with others with the joys of knowing Him and His Word. *Astounding!* The impact of their example altered my thinking forever about the importance of Bible reading as the obvious starting point for a life of service...and success.

### *The Reward of Reading the Bible*

And here's yet another instance of looking to and loving "this Book of the Law" and its reward. At our church was a young man whose father was diagnosed with terminal cancer. Immediately this caring son flew to be with his dad and to share the good news of eternal life through Christ. During that visit his father accepted

Christ as Savior and gave his heart and his life—what was left of it—to Him.

The dying man knew nothing about God and very little about Jesus. He wanted to know as much as he could about his Savior before he met Him personally in heaven. How could he learn about God and His Son? By reading His Word, of course! Not knowing how long he had to live, he devised a plan for reading through the Bible every week. His desire was to live wholly for God as long as God allowed him to live. By looking to the source of God's revelation to mankind on the pages of Scripture, this man gained daily rewards...until he entered glory some weeks later to gain the ultimate reward—seeing his Lord face-to-face!

## *The Divine Criteria for Success*

Why am I sharing these true examples? It's not to say, "Read through your Bible every week...or four times a year...or once a year...or read through a different translation of the Bible every year...or read 15 chapters a day." And certainly my message is not that you need to go to Bible school, a Bible institute, or a seminary. No, I want you to know the foundational element of success according to Joshua 1:8—"this Book of the Law." The Bible is the starting place for everything that matters, for all that really counts for success.

Remember, God is speaking to Joshua and giving him a new job assignment—to lead God's people into unfamiliar territory, to conquer it, to divide it, and to settle it. How will Joshua know if he's successful? And what is success? It's not wealth. It's not a title or a position. It's not what you own, who you know, or a list of accomplishments. And it's not being named in a *Who's Who* book. No, success according to God and as recorded in Joshua 1:8 is:

- knowing God's Word
- reading and studying God's Word
- thinking about God's Word

- obeying God's Word
- speaking God's Word
- following God's Word with all your heart

When we follow this divine criteria, we're succeeding in God's eyes and useful to Him for fulfilling His purposes. We may not measure up to the world's expectations or definitions of prospering, but God is well pleased.

### *God's Criteria for Success Lived Out*

One of my most delightful ministries over the years has been mentoring younger women. When we begin our meetings, I have each woman bring me her goals for her spiritual growth and for our time together. One woman's set of objectives still stands out in my mind. The college student wrote, "I want to read the Bible intelligently." *Intelligently.* She explained she didn't want to just tick off her Bible reading on a chart. She wanted comprehension—a grasp of what she read, why it was important enough to be in the Bible, and how it should impact her life.

I was thrilled because I once had a mentor who showed me how to read the Bible intelligently *and* live out its principles and teachings successfully. She was the same woman I mentioned earlier in this chapter, the one who read through her Bible four times each year. Here's her one added step, her bonus, her little bit of added motivation for picking up her Bible daily and diving in: Each time, before starting to read God's Word cover to cover, she chose a specific topic to watch for. Every day during her Bible time, she looked for a particular theme and journaled her findings in a special notebook.

My wise role model definitely read intelligently! So intelligently that the overflow of her time spent reading and learning about what God said on a number of topics led to many books authored by her. One quarter she looked for definitions and instances of integrity, and then she wrote a book on integrity. She did the same with time management. On the pages of Scripture she noted instance after instance of time and life management—instructions for using time wisely, examples of those who valued time and used it wisely, situations of those who foolishly wasted their hours, days, and years. She marked out principles for approaching each day and living it according to God's priorities and purposes.

I don't have to tell you this wonderful woman was successful in her life, her walk of integrity, her management of her time, her ministry, her mentoring of women, and her writing. She sought God's heart and mind about the issues of daily living, and then she followed Him and what she found in His Word with all her heart.

## *Moving Forward*

Moving forward sometimes means taking a look back. Stop for a minute and think about the women who've had the greatest influence on your Christian life. Like my models and mentors, they probably focused on the importance of God's Word. And, as they immersed themselves in the Bible—the source of all wisdom—they were able to offer you and others gems and principles of lasting value.

Isn't that the kind of person you want to be? That's the desire of my heart...and God's too. So where do you begin? What can you do to add God's Word—or more of it—into your already-too-busy life? Set a modest goal of reading a specific amount of God's Word daily. Then meditate on God's truths during the day.

I pray you're thinking about establishing a regular Bible time and finding a mentor to help you better know and live God's Word. The Bible is truly the starting point for any and all success. Are you experiencing a spark of excitement about God's Word? Great! Don't let the flame of desire for God's "Book of the Law" die. Stoke the coals! Fan the flame. Enjoy the blessings that are sure to come.

*Take the first step in faith.*
*You don't have to see the whole staircase,*
*just take the first step.*

Martin Luther King Jr.

# 3

# *The Road to Success*

*This Book of the Law shall not depart from your mouth,*
*but you shall meditate in it day and night,*
*that you may observe to do*
*according to all that is written in it.*
*For then you will make your way prosperous,*
*and then you will have good success.*

JOSHUA 1:8

One of my favorite definitions of success claims, "Success is living in such a way that you are using what God has given you—your intellect, abilities, and energy—to reach the purpose that He intends for your life."[1] Do you know people who live in such a way? Who use every single thing God's given them to the max? Who put what they have to full use and don't worry about what they don't have or let it stop them? Who make a difference and help others do the same?

## *Success Is Possible for Ordinary People*

Evidence abounds that Joshua is a marvelous example of an "average" person who enjoyed incredible success. He was:

- born a slave
- served as a subordinate until he was 50 years old

- fought bouts of fear
- required God's repeated encouragement in preparing to lead

Yet Joshua followed the formula at the beginning of this chapter—he used his divinely given assets, ultimately trusted God, lived boldly, and fulfilled God's plan and purpose for him. This ordinary man followed, served, and assisted Moses, God's mighty leader. After 40 years of faithful service, God selected Joshua to step into Moses' shoes and lead His people into the Promised Land.

### *Success Is Never Easy*

Joshua's road to success was not an easy one. He had to overcome a few speed-bumps—no, make that many major obstacles!—along the way:

- Joshua was the new leader on the block... expected to replace the great and awesome miracle-working Moses.
- The people Joshua was to lead were a mess—a ragtag group of fearful and obstinate whiners and complainers...numbering, according to some estimates, more than two million.
- Add to this the fierceness of the people who awaited the Israelites on the other side of the Jordan River, the enemies God's people would fight for many years before they could possess the land.

And that's only the beginning! After the major conquest through battle and until Joshua died, he was also to judge and instruct the people in matters of God's law.

How did an Egyptian slave become the conqueror of the Promised Land? How did a warrior become a discerner and teacher of the

Law of God? How did a humble and faithful follower and assistant become the powerful—and successful—leader of God's chosen people?

## *Success Comes from God*

Joshua's success is no secret. The answers to his advancement come to us in the first nine verses of Joshua, chapter 1. And to no one's surprise, the short answer is *God*. See for yourself the road to success...according to God.

- God spoke to Joshua (verse 1).
- God commanded Joshua to lead the people to their inheritance (verse 2).
- God assured Joshua of success every place his foot stepped (verse 3).
- God specifically defined the territory He promised the people (verse 4).
- God pledged His constant presence (verse 5).
- God encouraged Joshua personally and repeated His promise of the land (verse 6).
- God again encouraged Joshua and required him to explicitly follow His law (verse 7).
- God promised success to Joshua if he would speak, think, and follow all that was written in the Law (verse 8).
- God again warned Joshua not to be fearful but to obey His instructions and repeated His promise to be with Joshua every step of the way (verse 9).

God guided Joshua on His road to success. And here's good news! God will guide you too. His means of working in your life are the same as they were in Joshua's. God speaks and leads you through

His Word. He gives you His promises, instructs and encourages you along the way through His Word and His people, and accompanies you every step on the road of life.

Like Joshua, you can enjoy incredible success. But beware! Be prepared—it may not be the kind of success the world looks for and respects, such as wealth, fame, influential acquaintances, social standing, good looks, power, and prestige. You will live out God's plan and please Him as you study and obey His Word and follow Him with all your heart. And He will bless you in your efforts and service. That's His promise to you!

### *Following in Joshua's Footsteps*

Sometimes it's hard to follow the example of someone who lived thousands of years ago in a far-off country. So I'll ask: Do you know some Joshua-type women—women who follow God with all their hearts? Women who give much and risk much and do much for God's people and causes? I keep a list of Christian women I admire. When I get in a tight spot, when I feel too tired to go on, when things look hopeless, and when I wonder how I'm ever going to get everything done, take care of my responsibilities, find the energy to do what God and others ask of me, I think of these special, courageous, committed—and successful—women.

How can we, like Joshua and our Joshua-type women, carry out God's plan so He can use us to fulfill His will for us and the people around us as we contribute to His purposes? How can we do as Joshua did and conquer the challenges we run up against, mastering the roles and ministries God has in mind for us? How can we cross our Jordan Rivers—the barriers or fears or lacks that stand between us and the achievement of God's assignments?

Very simply, we need to follow in Joshua's footsteps. We need to know and obey God's Word as we pursue Him with all our hearts.

## *"God, Be in My Head"*

I certainly don't have the world's greatest voice, but I do love to sing, especially in a choir with lots of gifted singers around me. During my years in one church choir, we often sang a song and prayer entitled "God Be in My Head." It was one of the choir's—and the congregation's—favorites. Think about it. We love God and want to follow Him wholeheartedly. We delight to serve Him and His people. We relish the truths that we belong to Him, are in Him through His Spirit (Ephesians 1:13), and He is in us (Colossians 1:27), which means He is in our heads too. We should constantly keep Him in the forefront of our thoughts. This is the meaning of God's instruction to Joshua 1:8: "This Book of the Law shall not depart from your mouth." God is to be foremost in our minds, the One whom we think of first and always, the One we think of and seek to think like constantly.

So how can this become reality? How can we make God and His Word first in our hearts *and* our minds? As God told Joshua, the answer is simple—God's Word, the book of the law, is to be the focus of our daily lives. We are to put the Bible's truths into our minds, constantly meditating on the Bible day and night so we can apply its wisdom at all times and live according to all that is *in our heads*.

## *Reflecting on Truth*

Reflecting or meditating on God's Word is somewhat like my daily morning coffee-making routine. When the water in my coffee pot heats to a boil, it drains into and seeps through the grounds, drawing out the richness and flavor of the coffee. That's what meditation does for you. As you slowly read and simmer your way through a passage of scripture, the truths seep into your heart and mind. You begin to experience the richness of blessings from the living and abiding Word of God.

Meditation doesn't need to be limited to your quiet time either.

You can do as I've often done and write out verses on 3 x 5 cards that you take everywhere you go. One of my special "older women" made sure she had pockets in her slacks and skirts so she could carry verses with her to review while she was walking, driving, standing in lines, and waiting in medical offices. You can also recall and reflect on your special verses while you're getting ready for bed. Make God's Word your last thought as you drift off to sleep.

Meditation can also involve memorizing. That's what the psalmist described when he wrote, "Your word I have hidden in my heart" (Psalm 119:11). And that's what King David did. He wrote, "Delight yourself also in the LORD" (Psalm 37:4). David desired God's Word in his heart—not just in his hands and his house. There it could be taken or stolen. No, it had to be in his heart! He valued the law of the Lord and considered it a treasure worthy of being stored in the very core of his being. Only there would it be ready and available when he needed it.

I'm sure you've been told many times that you should read your Bible, memorize it, and meditate on it. Keep in mind that this instruction comes from God. You're probably thinking, *But I'm so busy! Where can I possibly find time to memorize and meditate on Scripture?* Maybe Joshua had similar thoughts. He was definitely a busy guy. But with all that was ahead of him, he couldn't afford *not* to be in God's Word—*deep* in God's Word. In the words of Bible scholar Matthew Henry, "If ever any man's business might have excused him from meditation, and other acts of devotion, one would think Joshua's might at this time in his life, as he stood on the brink of fierce, demanding battle."[2]

With God's Word in his head and heart, Joshua's first thoughts and his first words spoken as he began to lead, rule, and judge the matters of God's people would surely be God's Word. This would place Joshua on God's road to success. And he would be leading God's people down that same road.

## *Digging into the Truth*

God's path to sure success in our many responsibilities, endeavors, and challenges involves loving, revering, memorizing, and reflecting on His Word, on "this Book of the Law," on the Bible. In Joshua's day, the Word of the Lord was delivered to Moses written in stone. Moses then read it out loud to the people, including Joshua. Now it was Joshua's turn to keep it alive for the Israelites, which required that it be in him—in his head, *alive* in his heart, *quick* on his tongue, and his *constant diet* for his soul.

"This Book of the Law shall not depart from your mouth," God instructed Joshua. In other words, when the people had a matter for judgment, Joshua was to base his decision on God's law alone. No other precepts were to come out of his mouth. God put His law in Joshua's hand, and he was to conform every act of his leadership and ruling to it.

How could this happen for Joshua? And, more personally, how can this happen for you and me today? Well, what held true for Joshua still holds true for us today. We must read, reflect on, and memorize God's truth...but we also must dig deep into it for understanding and application.

If Step 1 on God's highway to success is meditating and memorizing God's Word, Step 2 is studying it. It's one thing to read the Bible and even memorize parts or verses of it. But we can recite the Bible and not understand it! Our goal should be to examine and analyze the Bible *until we grasp its meanings.*

> *Do you love God's Word? Are you passionate about becoming better acquainted with its truths?*

Someone once pointed out that Bible reading is like flying over a jungle in an airplane and looking down. You see a river, a plantation here, a forest there, and the roads going through it. You're seeing the whole. But Bible study is like personally walking the roads through that same territory, that same jungle, and handling each leaf or touching each tree, crossing the river and getting wet, experiencing every detail of the terrain.

How are you reacting to the thought of "studying"? Did you think your schooldays were over? Oh, please don't! Devote time and attention to gaining knowledge, to analyzing, to reading with deliberate and careful effort God's Word.

My daughters love to cook. They're on the Internet daily, downloading recipes, and they watch and record cooking programs on TV. But one of my daughters took her love for food preparation to the next level by taking cooking classes at a famous culinary institute in the Denver area. She studied the art and science of cooking. Study comes down to *interest* and *desire*. Like my super busy daughter, if you love something intensely enough, you'll do whatever it takes—spend whatever money it takes, give whatever amount of time it takes—to become better acquainted with it.

Do you love God's Word? Are you passionate about becoming better acquainted with its truths? Do you long to please God and really live His plan for you? Then what are you waiting for? Follow Paul's admonition: "Be diligent to present yourself approved to God, a worker who does not need to be ashamed, rightly dividing the word of truth" (2 Timothy 2:15).

Opportunities to study the Bible are everywhere. Join a Bible-study group, enter into a mentoring relationship, enroll in classes (day or night) at church or in homes, attend a Bible institute or college. I began digging into God's truths through Moody Bible Correspondence School. As a busy young mom with two preschool girls, I worked away on book after book of the Bible, here a lesson, there a lesson, while my little ones napped.

And in my mentoring ministry I encourage other young moms to do the same. I tell them, "You *can* be growing while you raise your family." And bonuses abound for taxed, overworked, overstressed moms as their studies lead to possessing God's patience, having peace in their hearts—even on the craziest of days!—and experiencing God's wisdom as they deal with the difficult situations marriage and parenting sometimes entail.

And the same is true on the other end of life. As you grow in your maturity of knowing God and understanding His Word, you're better prepared to face the twilight years, as your body deteriorates. You can walk with confidence as you pass through "the valley of the shadow of death" (Psalm 23). You can and will fear no evil. Why? Because God is with you. He's your rod and your staff, your comforter (Psalm 23:4). And that's a promise!

### *Mary, Jesus' Mother*

I've talked a lot about Joshua, but my mind is racing toward a Joshua-type woman—Mary, who became the mother of Jesus. Mary had no glowing background that we know of. Her parents are never mentioned. She appears on the pages of Scripture as a young woman, probably a teenager. Mary was the woman who, after she heard the shepherds' story and the angels' message about her Son, "kept all these things and pondered them in her heart" (Luke 2:19). She also hid God's Word in her heart and meditated on it because when she spoke what's now known as her "Magnificat" (Luke 1:46-55), she used Scripture, reciting from memory *with understanding*. She obviously had studied and been taught Scripture. At least 15 references of Scripture are cited or referred to within the 10 verses that poured from her heart to God's heart.

Mary was by no means successful in the eyes of the world. Yet she accepted God's plan to be the vessel to bring His Son into the world. God's Word was in her heart and in her head. And it was on her tongue. This knowledge gave her the courage to step into God's will, to give and to give up all to follow God with a complete heart. It cost her dearly in the eyes of people—she was pregnant without being married, considered a fornicator (John 8:41). She would be hunted down by those who wanted to murder her infant Son, and later she suffered as she watched Him die on the cross.

However, in the eyes of *God,* Mary was favored, chosen, and sought out. And she was blessed by Him. In her "Magnificat," Mary praises God, who is mighty and had done great things for her (Luke 1:49). Truly, in God's eyes, she was successful.

## *Moving Forward*

Oh dear. I'm another voice telling you to read, study, and memorize Scripture. But it's wonderful! To have God in your head and His Word in your heart to empower you to follow Him and His plan for you with all your heart, soul, strength, and mind, you must actively and decisively put it there.

As you consider the simplicity and repetition of these steps to spiritual growth, realize they're dynamite. When you look at the words on paper, you may want to yawn and say, "Yeah, sure, what's new?" Maybe you'll even think, *I tried reading the Bible before. I've done a stint or two of Bible study. And I was in a program once where I memorized some verses. I don't feel like doing any of this right now.* But don't forget these are *spiritual* principles, *spiritual* disciplines.

No matter how my words look, or whether or not you've tried to implement these practices before, when you allow God's Word to "dwell in you richly" (Colossians 3:16), things happen. Wonderful things! Amazing things! Even things you don't understand and can't understand or explain. You'll discover fresh energy, new excitement, and a different—and better—outlook on life. Your goals *will* change. I guarantee it. You'll dream of doing great things for God as you begin to understand what great things He has done for *you.* You'll have ideas and wonder, *Now where did those come from?* You'll treat people differently, treat them better. You'll find yourself embracing and tackling your ministries, work, and responsibilities with joy! You won't even recognize yourself.

Bottom line? You'll be traveling God's road to success, tasting and partaking of His brand of achievement and contribution. Why? Because you chose to do as He instructed you and Joshua. You meditated on God's Word day and night. You chose to breathe, think, ponder, relish, and live God's book of the law.

*Let us not be content to wait and*
*see what will happen,*
*but give us the determination to*
*make the right things happen.*

Peter Marshall

4

# A Sure Recipe for Success

*This Book of the Law shall not depart from your mouth,*
*but you shall meditate in it day and night,*
*that you may observe to do*
*according to all that is written in it.*
*For then you will make your way prosperous,*
*and then you will have good success.*

JOSHUA 1:8

My husband, Jim, has traveled the world for various ministries. I'm constantly fascinated by his many tales of adventure and fruitful sharing of the gospel and helping others. Each of his trips included blessings and challenges. After one particular journey to China some years ago with a group of seminary students, Jim told me about one student who was always gone when the group was preparing to move to its next location. Security was extremely strict, and the guide responsible for keeping the group on schedule was close to having a nervous breakdown by the time the classmates left the country...mainly due to this one student. The young man was so enthralled with the culture that he often forgot to follow instructions. (Now, before you think too poorly of him, you'll be happy to know that not too long after the China trip, he met and married a young woman after God's own heart and today they are missionaries to an Asian country.)

## *Following Instructions*

"What does this story about the 'missing' young man have to do with following God with all your heart, with success, or even with the life of Joshua?" Everything! Why? Because following instructions—also known as obedience—is the third ingredient in God's recipe for your success in living out His plan for you. So far we've considered these ingredients for success, all drawn from Joshua 1:8:

> Ingredient #1: *Believing God's Word*—This book of the law, the Bible, is God's recipe book. You need to believe that the Bible is "living and powerful" (Hebrews 4:12) and able to make a difference in lives, including yours.
>
> Ingredient #2: *Dwelling on God's Word*—You need to meditate in it day and night. You cannot correctly follow what you don't understand. The Bible must be understood by your mind before it can move your heart and change your life.

And now we come to ingredient #3: *Obeying God's Word*—You need to observe and do according to all that is written in it.

## *Obeying God's Word*

Everything we've discussed to this point about success has focused on *internals.* The successful woman in God's eyes knows God's Word in her heart by reading and meditating on it. Now we move to the *externals.* And for many, this is where following God starts to get sticky. It's easy to read about a subject or principle or, in this case, the commands in Scripture. But now comes the harder step. You see, *there's something we must do,* and that's obey God's Word. Not just the parts that are easy…or the ones we like…or the commands that won't cramp our style. No, we need to obey *all* of them!

God promised Joshua success on one condition—that he obey the book of God's law. Woven into the sovereign design of success is the condition of obedience. If Joshua would magnify God's Word with his lips and edify his soul by continually meditating on the precepts of the Word, then there would be fruit. And that fruit takes the form of obedience. What's inside will come out. We can reverse this truth: If a person isn't obedient, then the Word of God probably doesn't have a very high place in his or her life and devotion.

Remember all those responsibilities and tasks we've been talking about? The work, the roles, the job assignments God has given to us? In these we're to be obedient. In our service to others and the church, we're to be obedient. In the careful tending to our walk with God, we're to be obedient. In our manner of speech, we're to be obedient. On and on the list goes. A line from a hymn I love, "Blessed Assurance," reads, "Perfect submission, all is at rest." If we're obedient—in "perfect submission"—we are blessed.

## *How Not to Succeed*

Everyone has his or her own idea about how to succeed. Sadly, it's just that—the person's own idea. One group who chose not to do things God's way was the Israelites. Not long after the children of Israel left Egypt, they were challenged by Joshua and Caleb to enter the Promised Land. The reason it was a challenge was because the other 10 spies sent to scope out the area gave an extremely negative account on the wisdom of attacking because of the strength of the enemy on the other side of the Jordan River. They reported, "All the people whom we saw in it are men of great stature. There we saw the giants..." (Numbers 13:32-33).

Well, that was just what the people didn't need or want to hear. They were at a crossroad. They could weep and cry all night and wish they'd stayed in Egypt...or they could trust God, follow Joshua, and step into God's plan. Joshua and his friend Caleb reasoned with them:

> If the LORD delights in us, then He will bring us into this land and give it to us...Only do not rebel against the LORD, nor fear the people of the land...their protection has departed from them, and the LORD is with us. Do not fear them (Numbers 14:8-9).

*When we disregard God's Word, disobey Him, or fail to believe in His promises, we experience defeat.*

Sadly, the Israelites had their own ideas about the best choice: "All the congregation said to stone them" (verse 10). If the Lord hadn't intervened, Joshua and Caleb would have been murdered!

The Israelites' disobedience and rebellious attitude resulted in their dying in the wilderness over the next 40 years. Their lack of trust in God and their failure to follow His Word as relayed to them by Joshua resulted in their defeat. They never reached the Promised Land...although their descendants did.

Dear friend, the same is true for you and me today. Any time we disregard God's Word, disobey Him, or fail to believe His promises, we experience defeat. We miss God's will. And, tragically, we miss out on many of His great and precious promises (2 Peter 1:4). We reap the opposite of success.

### *Tasting God's Success*

The simple recipe God outlined for Joshua for gaining sure success goes against everything the world factors into a success formula. Most people judge others first by their beauty and looks, including the clothes and jewelry they wear. They want to know job titles and annual incomes. They move next to the kinds of houses the people own and the cars they drive. But Joshua followed God's recipe and added massive quantities of the ingredients He called for. Joshua turned his back on the world and its measuring cup for success. He followed God's instructions to the letter, and it sure worked! If his accomplishments—his successes—were listed in a *Who's Who* book, you'd read about these awesome achievements.

*Joshua was successful against his enemies.* Soon after God's people crossed the Red Sea while leaving Egyptian slavery, Israel was attacked by a fierce group of nomads—the Amalekites. Moses asked Joshua to lead a group of untrained soldiers into battle. Joshua was probably fearful and unsure of himself and his ragtag army, but he was also obedient. And God gave Joshua a stunning victory (Exodus 17:8-13).

When you run up against enemies and obstacles, trust God and fulfill His will. When you have your moments of weakness and doubt, look up, believe in God's plan and His promises, and move forward! You'll never know success without taking that first step of obedience. Success is often as simple as taking a first step.

*Joshua was successful in battle.* This time Joshua was asked to conquer an evil, violent people under ever more overwhelming odds. Moses, the great Israelite leader, was dead. Joshua was asked to lead an attack with his untrained army against an even greater foe than the Amalekites. God assigned Joshua to invade a land with numerous fortified cities and well-armed and battle-ready fighters. Again Joshua obeyed and God gave him victory (Joshua 3–12). In fact, Joshua was so successful in invading and conquering the land that military strategists today study his approaches to battle.

Think again about your assignments from God. Are you approaching your tasks with God's leading, like Joshua did, or are you going it alone? Doing it your way? Are you in a battle with a noncommunicative teen who's withdrawn from the family? Who maybe wants nothing to do with God and His Son? Is there a marital problem, a husband who's less than excited about fulfilling his assignments from God? Are there problems and problem people at work? Look to God's Word, find out what He says you're to do, follow Joshua's example, and do what God says—and do it His way. You will reap success, even if that success is simply knowing you obeyed the Lord.

*Joshua was successful in his assignments.* For Joshua, battles were only the beginning. There were stepping-stones time after time toward the primary assignment God had for him—he was to implement God's promise to give His people an inheritance. Humanly speaking, we would say Joshua's assignment was impossible. Each of the 12 tribes who made up the mass of God's people had its own band of leaders, its own tribal culture, and its own ideas. Envision trying to manage this diverse crowd and attempting to please two million-plus new home owners, all of whom wanted property with water and the best views and, of course, maximum curb appeal (Joshua 13–19). And yet Joshua was unwavering in his commitment to his assignment. He followed through. He obeyed. And he finished his assignment...successfully!

*We must believe in God's plan for us, lock in on it, move forward, see it through, and finish. Then we'll know God's brand of success.*

Joshua's assignment from God was long-term and involved. It was demanding...and extremely trying. If your "assignments" are anything like mine and most of the women I know, they look daunting too. But we have the same God as Joshua... and the same promises from Him. We, like Joshua, must listen and adhere to everything God tells us. We must believe in His plan for us, lock in on it, move forward, see it through, and finish. *Then* we will know God's brand of success.

*Joshua was successful in his personal life.* There's no doubt Joshua was a key person in the conquest of the land. On top of that, he diplomatically managed the next-to-impossible job of dividing the land among the 12 tribes of Israel. That's great, isn't it? But Joshua was also *personally* successfully. He experienced personal pleasure in the satisfaction of a job well done. He enjoyed fulfillment for his efforts, labor, and decades of faithful obedience. And perhaps best of all, he knew in his heart others benefited because of his obedience. The people were genuinely grateful and, to show their appreciation, they rose up as a group, honored him, and gave him the city he asked for as his allotment in the land (Joshua 19:49-50).

You too will be blessed when you, like Joshua, dedicate yourself to God's requirements for success. When you do your best and give your all to follow God with all your heart, you'll know the Lord's "well done, good and faithful servant." When you continue on and diligently see a project through to the end, you'll relish a sense of fulfillment that only God's brand of success can produce. And blessing upon blessings, you will bless others as well!

## *Obedience 101*

Reflecting back on Joshua's successes—an obvious result of his obedience to God—I have a question to ask. It's one I ask for myself in prayer each day as I talk things over with God. "Is there any area in your life where you are not obeying the Lord?" I don't save such soul searching for Sunday church. I ask this question about me daily. Twenty-four hours is a long time…and a lot can happen in the Sin Department in those hours. So to be a woman who follows God with all my heart, I make every effort to keep a clean account with God.

One day a woman approached me at church, handed me a piece

of paper, and said, "I know you're interested in this kind of thing, and I wanted you to have this." Across the top of the page was the title: "Questions to Ask Yourself Each Day." One of the questions pierced my heart: "Are all my relationships made right?" Friend, that is a life-changing question if you ask it with an obedient heart each morning and again each evening when you put your head on your pillow. I encourage you to include this in your daily soul searching.

If God reveals a problem between you and another person or some slight malice or anger on your part toward someone, something must be done. And if you ask, "Is there any area in my life where I am not obeying You, Lord?" and know in your heart there is, then something must be done. This is Obedience 101.

Let's face it. We don't want to fail or like failure. Admitting sin is painful. But it's also a mandatory step of obedience God asks of us. As Christ stated, "If you love Me, keep My commandments" (John 14:15). With obedience to God comes joy...and God's blessing...and God's type of success. A successful woman *knows* God's Word, *loves* God's Word, and *lives* God's Word. These are the keys to success in the spiritual realm, which will spill over into the day-to-day practical realm. The best measure of spiritual life is not how emotional you are about the things of the Lord, even though emotions are important. No, it's how obedient you are.

## *Moving Forward*

To move forward in your desire to follow God with all your heart, emulate Joshua's devotion. He loved God, and he loved the book of the law. In Joshua is a very straightforward example of how you can achieve success God's way. The Lord is showing you where you can find the courage and hope of victory and the wisdom necessary for fulfilling your responsibilities. Joshua's faithfulness to God's careful instructions reveals the way. If you love God, follow Him, and obey His holy Word, you will be successful in the eyes of God—and that's all that truly matters!

How can you get this success formula operating for you?

- ✓ *Reexamine* your life according to the three key components to success: your heart for God's Word, your heart for thinking on God's Word, and your heart for obeying God's Word.
- ✓ *Relinquish* how you may have defined success in the past and allow God to redesign your values.
- ✓ *Reflect* on your level of obedience. Have you been as careful as you should be in doing what the Bible says?
- ✓ *Realign* your practices and values to demonstrate the perspective and level of obedience God desires.
- ✓ *Realize* the impact of your obedience. What is God asking you to do? Obeying makes a huge difference, beyond what you can think of or dream of. Imagine what the world would be like if…

Noah had said, "I don't do boats."
David had said, "I don't do Goliaths."
Mary had said, "I don't do virgin births."
John the Baptist had said, "I don't do baptisms."
Paul had said, "I don't do letters."
Jesus had said, "I don't do crosses!"[1]

And what if…

Joshua had said, "I don't cross Jordans."

# Section 2

# *Becoming a Courageous Woman*

*If it is [God's] plan that we should*
*march through a river,*
*or attack a walled town, or turn*
*to fight an army,*
*we have simply to go forward.*
*He will make the mountains [go] away.*
*Rivers will dry up; walls will fall down;*
*armies shall be scattered.*

F.B. Meyer

# 5

# *Focusing for Greatness*

*Have I not commanded you?*
*Be strong and of good courage;*
*do not be afraid, nor be dismayed,*
*for the* LORD *your God is with you*
*wherever you go.*

JOSHUA 1:9

I'm so excited! In one week I get to travel to the Grand Canyon to speak at a women's conference. I'm thrilled about the event and the wonderful women I'll meet. But I also can't stop thinking about the first time I saw this unbelievable, immense gorge and geological wonder—the *Grand* Canyon. Our trip happened when Jim and I were moving to California. Our drive took us within 60 miles of this world-famous canyon. We were so tired we almost didn't go to the canyon's rim, but we decided we would. Oh, I'm so glad we did!

I vividly remember standing beside Jim at the lookout point, hand in hand, in utter awe. From our vantage point we spotted a little string of water a mile below us. We read on the information plaque that it was the Colorado River, the second longest river in the United States—running for 2,000 miles. It is so powerful that if you stood at one point and looked at it for 24 hours, a million tons of sand, silt, gravel, and boulders, not to mention water would go past. And it all *raged* by. And yet in some places this river is only 12 feet deep.

*How could such a small trickle of water have the force and power of such magnitude that it could carve out, in time, a mile-deep, vast gorge?* we wondered. The answer lies in the walls of the canyon. Without the vertical embankments on each side to restrict, guide, and channel this relatively little flow of water, the water would be just a lake. With the walls…well, with them the world has a wonder.

I hope you're holding your breath and hanging on to something because Joshua 1:9 introduces you to the force and power your life possesses when you channel it between the two immovable walls God erects for guiding you and giving you power as you move toward living His plan for you.

### *Power Can Come in Small Packages*

Force. Power. Magnificent and amazing. That's what I want my life to be and to illustrate. A marvel that evidences hidden energy and influence. A wonder that can't be explained…except by and because of God.

As I think about being a woman, I realize the Bible describes women as "the weaker vessel" or "the weaker partner" (1 Peter 3:7 NKJV and NIV). Yet any woman, however weak or small, limited or deprived, can have a mighty effect that causes others to stop, take notice, marvel, and glorify God. Like the ribbon-like Colorado River at the bottom of the Grand Canyon, we can make a remarkable difference and do astonishing things for God.

How?

By living the life lessons found in Joshua 1:8-9. By doing as Joshua did. By taking God at His Word. By believing in His promises. By acting on His will. By counting on His presence. By putting feet and wings on our faith in God. And by following Him with all our hearts…no matter what.

It works like this. God gives us a command—something He wants us to do and expects us to do. And it's scary...or difficult... or it looks impossible...or maybe we feel exhausted already. We know He wants us to do it. So our choices begin right then and there. Will we do it or not? Will we make the effort or not? Will we even try? Will we, like Joshua, "arise, go over this Jordan" (Joshua 1:2), whatever it is and whatever it entails? Look again at Joshua 1, verse 9:

> Have I not commanded you? Be strong and of good courage; do not be afraid, nor be dismayed, for the LORD your God is with you wherever you go.

## *The Road to Success*

We'll get to verse 9 in a while, but first take a quick look back. In the previous section we dove into Joshua 1:8, referred to by Dwight L. Moody, a famous preacher from the past, as "God's instruction for Bible study." There we discovered the factors that go into success as conveyed by God to His servant, Joshua. We learned what makes a woman successful in God's eyes:

- She diligently grows in her knowledge of God and His Word.
- She faithfully hides God's Word in her heart.
- She carefully thinks on God's Word at all times and in every situation.
- She thoroughly carries out God's Word through obedience.

The result? Success. Prosperity. A life of inner peace, of favor and blessing, of contribution and meaning. And a life of courage, confidence, and fierce commitment. Now we turn to Joshua 1:9. We're to move forward with courage because God is with us.

## *Following God...No Matter What*

Who can we look to as examples of success and power in their endeavors for God? People with these characteristics:

- an unexplainable power in what they did and said
- obvious wisdom in their words
- clarity of vision and purpose
- abundant strength and energy for the tasks in front of them, whether a daily, monotonous one or a special challenge.

As you read about some role models for us, don't fail to note that almost to a person their success and power came in the midst of pain and adversity. Yet each took steps of faith and courage as they wholeheartedly trusted God, followed Him into the unknown, and, in most cases, into the unpleasant.

*Joseph*—Success isn't something that just happens. As Charles Swindoll puts it, "Success is when preparation meets opportunity." Joseph is one of the greatest success stories in the Bible. His story is recorded in Genesis 37–50. But his success wasn't without struggle. Sold into slavery by 10 jealous brothers reduced Joseph, the spoiled, favorite son of the biblical patriarch Jacob, to a lowly servant in the household of an Egyptian official and later a prisoner in chains (Genesis 39:1,20).

These situations didn't keep Joseph from succeeding. First he "found favor" in the eyes of his Egyptian master (Genesis 39:4). Then, when he was unjustly treated, God "gave him favor in the sight of the keeper of the prison" where he was incarcerated due to a lie (verse 21). And Joseph's wise suggestions after interpreting Pharaoh's dreams brought him favor in the eyes of both Pharaoh and his advisors (Genesis 41:37).

How did such success happen? Joseph's integrity and hard work in the midst of hardship met with favor in God's eyes. Even being alone, in a faraway and different country, forced to be a servant and prisoner, Joseph followed God with all his heart...no matter what. God blessed Joseph's attitude and work, which was noticed by everyone around him. Joseph's focus on pleasing God resulted in him becoming second in command to the mighty Egyptian Pharaoh, positioning Joseph to save God's people when famine struck (Genesis 50:20).

*Daniel*—A privileged young man until taken captive by the Babylonians, Daniel never returned to his family or homeland (Daniel 1:3-6). Like Joseph, he had a choice regarding how to respond. He could have become angry, depressed, discouraged, or dejected. But, also like Joseph, he chose to focus his attention on God and be and do the best he could at what was asked of him in his undesirable situation (verses 8,18-20). Daniel faithfully (and uncompromisingly!) served three different heathen kings, spanning some 70 years and two empires. King Nebuchadnezzar, the first king, rewarded Daniel for his efforts and "gave him many great gifts" and "made him ruler over the whole province of Babylon, and chief administrator over all the wise men of Babylon" (2:48).

How did this power and success happen? In a word: *God*. God "brought Daniel into the favor and goodwill of the chief of the eunuchs" (Daniel 1:9). Daniel's miraculous survival in the lions' den was because "the God of Daniel...delivered Daniel from the power of the lions" testified King Darius (6:26-27). Daniel spent a lifetime focused on God and courageously doing His will...no matter what.

*Esther*—Taken from her home and put into the harem of the great king of Persia, the beautiful Esther was in a terrible situation. But like others who shine bright as examples of those who rose above their difficult circumstances, God was at work in, through, and on behalf of this Hebrew woman. Because of God and Esther's gentle spirit, "the young woman pleased [the custodian of the women], and she obtained his favor." She also "obtained favor in the sight of all who saw her." Plus "the king loved Esther more than all the other women, and she obtained grace and favor in his sight...so he set the royal crown upon her head and made her queen" (Esther 2:9,15,17).

Esther's courage and character—no matter where or in what conditions—were blessed by God. In His great providence, God gave her success, which secured her the position of queen. As queen she later influenced the king and saved the lives of God's people living in that country (7:3; 9:24-25).

*Ruth*—Scan the book of Ruth and you're in for a treat. A stranger in a strange land, the young widow Ruth won the hearts and admiration of an entire village. After her husband's death and the death of her father-in-law, Ruth chose to take the bold step of leaving her country and family to go with her mother-in-law Naomi and embrace Naomi's God. She followed Naomi and God with all her heart and journeyed to Bethlehem (Ruth 1:22).

About Ruth's attitude, efforts, and work ethic, well-respected businessman Boaz said, "It has been fully reported to me, all that you have done for your mother-in-law." Boaz also noted, "All the people of my town know that you are a virtuous woman." The women in town also took notice of Ruth's heart of devotion and reminded Naomi, "Your daughter-in-law, who loves you...is better to you than seven sons" (Ruth 2:11; 3:11; 4:15).

God's favor and blessing elevated this young widow, who gleaned in the fields for food for Naomi and herself, to the position of wife to the prosperous landowner Boaz. Boaz and Ruth had a son, Obed. And Obed became the grandfather of David in the line of Jesus Christ, the Messiah and Savior of all who trust in Him.

*Mary, the mother of Jesus*—Young Mary was blessed by all generations (Luke 1:48; I encourage you to read Mary's story that begins in Luke 1:1). She was chosen and graced by God to become the human vessel—the mother—who became pregnant via the Holy Spirit and bore God's Son and our Savior Jesus Christ into the world. This much-desired role could only be given to one woman in the history of mankind, and that woman was one who followed God with all her heart. And so it was that Mary was "highly favored" and "found favor with God" (verses 28 and 30). What merited such high praise? It wasn't her hard work or pleasing disposition. No, it was a tribute to her inner person, which is expressed in her "Magnificat," her song to God when her heart for Him overflowed into praise (verses 46-55).

We don't know Mary's age, but she was probably in her teens when God announced His plan for her life. With a heart of faith she courageously followed Him into His will…even when she didn't understand it. Mary stands as an example of success—the careful preparation of a lowly life and a devoted heart of obedience embracing God's invitation to be the one who is "blessed" among all women (verse 28) even as she faced struggles and sorrow. God honored her heart and selected this young woman who considered herself a "maidservant of the Lord" and "lowly" (verses 38 and 48). As Mary stated, God puts down the mighty and exalts the lowly (verse 52).

## *Moving Forward*

There's one more success story to share—*yours!* When you, like this lineup of God-followers, focus your heart, soul, mind, and strength on God and His Word, you'll experience God's kind of success. Through His Word, God reveals His will to you and gives you the power you need to accomplish the jobs He has for you.

How can you move forward in your desire to be a more courageous woman? How can you march through whatever river is impeding your progress, attack whatever hindrances appear, and fight your enemies?

*The truths in God's Word must be first and foremost in your mind and heart.* They need to be the ruler of your every thought, word, and deed. After all, the Bible is for *you*—to edify you. It's not here to prepare you for ministry and service (although it definitely does!). And it's not here to earn you any kind of award, certificate, or recognition for the number of verses you memorize (although that can't hurt, and it certainly can help). No, it's here to build *you* up, to change *you,* to teach *you* God's ways, to show *you* God's will, and to empower *you* to move forward with courage.

*Let the power and force of God's Word energize you!*

*Take care that your focus is in the right place...and on the right Person.* Fix your focus on God...not on your problems. On His commands...not your confusion. On His presence...not your fears. Serve Him, trust Him, and count on Him. After the psalmist wondered, "Where does my help come from?" he answered, "My help comes from the LORD" (Psalm 121:1-2 NIV). You have God's commands (His will) and God's presence. What more do you need?

When energized by His force and power, you can follow God with all your *heart* and accomplish the tasks He gives you and calls you to. You can fulfill all you have to do daily and throughout life... no matter what. That's God's definition of greatness! You can lead your children, help your husband, serve in ministry, assist others, and successfully live out God's will and plan for you. God's Word *is* force and power—the power for accomplishing His will...no matter where or in what circumstances. *With God as your focus you will be strong and courageous!*

*There is no such thing as*
*impossibility when God says,*
*"Forward, soul; arise, go over this Jordan!"*

F.B. Meyer

# 6

# *Facing the Impossible*

*Have I not commanded you?*
*Be strong and of good courage;*
*do not be afraid, nor be dismayed,*
*for the LORD your God is with you*
*wherever you go.*

JOSHUA 1:9

In my biblical counseling days more than one woman came to me with complaints that ended with something like this: "I can't make this work, so why try? It's impossible!" These women had either given in or given up (or maybe given out). They'd determined that *it* (whatever *it* was) simply couldn't be done: "My marriage can't be fixed." "My kids can't be helped." "I could never take on this ministry." "My problem can't be solved." On and on went their lists of impossible situations they had no hope or solutions for.

What these women, and you and I, can do immediately is take advantage of God's admonition to Joshua: "Be strong and of good courage." Like Joshua, who was leading God's people into the Promised Land, we have a need to be steadfast and courageous as we look our issues and God-given roles, jobs, and opportunities in the eye. Also, like Joshua, we need to remember that *the LORD our God is with us wherever we go.* Nothing is ever as bad or as impossible as it seems when we realize God is with us in everything we face.

## *Seven Habits for Gaining Strength and Courage*

God tells Joshua that his problems are not *problems* but actually a need for strength in facing his *opportunities:*

> Have I not commanded you? Be strong and of good courage; do not be afraid, nor be dismayed, for the LORD your God is with you wherever you go (Joshua 1:9).

Be strong, Joshua! "Strengthen yourself, encourage yourself, harden yourself, behave valiantly, and take courage. You can do this because I am with you!" God says, in essence.

As I thought about being strong in the Lord—single-minded, unwavering, full of faith—I had to give an all-knowing nod and utter "Ah, yes!" I totally related to any and all *opposite responses*...until I grasped the concept of *being* strong. You see, my routine starts about the same every day. I wake up—usually before the alarm goes off—and my mind goes crazy. Going back to sleep is pretty much impossible. My mind is like a little recording that starts with the same song every day: "I have so much to do! In fact, I have *too* much to do! I'll never get it all done!" In the past, before learning about Joshua 1:9, my mental process concluded, "So why try? After all, it's impossible. Why bother to even try to do any of it?"

But thanks to God's firmness and emphatic instructions to be strong and fearless, I've been toughening up mentally. I started making it a habit to go ahead and be strong in Christ (no matter what my busy, impossible day, work, or challenges looked like). I began purposefully wading into my own Jordan River, boldly taking the first step into my impossible days. And I adopted seven habits that continue to help me find phenomenal, unexplainable strength for actively living God's will. Then and only then do I have a chance of becoming like the Colorado River, which began its erosion effect and kept on rolling as it carved out the Grand Canyon...and continues to do so.

1. *Know God's character.* If you turn in your Bible to Numbers 14:9, you'll discover that by the age of 40 Joshua was understanding a few things about God's character. God had promised His people victory, and Joshua encouraged the disgruntled masses by saying, "Do not rebel against the LORD, nor fear the people of the land, for they are our bread; their protection has departed from them, and the LORD is with us. Do not fear them."

God had given and would continue to give His people victory. The Lord's very nature couldn't and wouldn't allow Him to go back on His promises. Joshua could go into battle with courage and strength of purpose, knowing God had assured him of victory. God wasn't going to let him down or let him fail.

This same understanding of God's character will give you confidence too. God has promised His presence and assured you of ultimate victory. So be confident as you walk through each day, as you seek to follow God wholeheartedly. The apostle Paul put it this way, "Thanks be to God who *always* leads us in triumph in Christ" (2 Corinthians 2:14). Do you believe this? Then trust God as you face and fight your battles.

2. *Embrace God's plan for you.* God gave Joshua a clear, specific, mammoth job assignment. The task ahead of him would not be easy, but he knew what he had to do. And God has given you and me assignments too. In my case...

> *Scene 1:* I'm a wife. This means the human care of my husband falls on me. Jim is my highest *human* priority. He is the top person or matter on my daily to-do list. Loving and caring for Jim is God's will for me. It's where my second effort and energy need to be used (my first effort is for God!).

In her book *Let Me Be a Woman,* Elisabeth Elliot writes, "When you make a choice, you accept the limitations of that choice. To accept limitations requires maturity. To do this, is not to do that. To be this, is not to be that. So, to be married, is not to be single. Which may mean not to have a career." Mrs. Elliot also said, "To marry this man is not to marry all the others."[1] (And, I would add, it is not to even *look* at the others.)

Choice is a limitation in itself. So when you marry, you get a new job assignment. You can fight and chafe against your assignment or you can yield to it, accepting that it comes from God and knowing that it represents His path for your life. You can give your marriage your all, knowing you're following God's will. And don't forget what God promised in Joshua 1:8: "Then you will be prosperous and successful" (NIV). (Devoting ourselves fully to our marriages and our husbands is the path to blessings that are immeasurable, indescribable, and limitless. It's the road to success.)

> *Scene 2:* When Jim and I became parents, I received yet another job assignment from the Lord—to be the best mom I could be. Sure, I loved my new baby to pieces! But suddenly I had an additional sacrifice. Not only was I to sacrifice for my husband, but now I tasted what it means to sacrifice for a child, to set aside other things (for decades!) and dedicate those years to care for, train, nurture, and raise our child. And when our daughter was an infant, who got up in the middle of the night when she cried or had a need? Who gave up her (I started to write "his or her," but we both know who it usually was, don't we?) right to a good night's sleep? And then Jim and I had another daughter so the needed sacrifices increased. When the kids got older, who slept with one eye and ear open until she knew everyone was home from work, classes, studies, and time with friends? And when the nest was empty, who took on the nurturing of long-distance relationships? You

know the answer, don't you? Me...and you at your house...because we're moms!

One Bible mom, Hannah, shows us the success of focus and strength (read her inspiring story in 1 Samuel, chapters 1 and 2). Hannah had a difficult assignment. To begin with, she was a devoted wife to Elkanah. Her life and marriage were tough challenges because there was another wife. This second wife bore Elkanah sons, but Hannah was barren for many years. Finally God granted Hannah's wish, and a child and a situation that called for unusual commitment came. God gave Hannah and Elkanah little Samuel, whom they raised and diligently taught him about God for three years... right up to the second they handed their preschooler to the priest to be raised by him in the temple—as Hannah had promised to God. Yes, Hannah had a harder than usual assignment. But she obeyed God in every way. She kept the law, kept the Nazarite vow she took, and kept her promise to God to give little Samuel back to Him for a lifetime of service.

When Christians today look for an excellent role-model mother, many think first of Hannah. In fact, I have a research volume that labels Hannah "the woman who personifies ideal motherhood."[2] And how does Hannah's story end? After following God's recipe for success and strengthening herself with courage all the way through leaving her child with a priest, Hannah had five more children! She devoted herself to them, all the while carrying on a long-distance relationship with her first son. Hannah was a successful and courageous mom. And Samuel became a successful and courageous

*Like the Colorado River carving the Grand Canyon, something magnificent comes from funneling your life between the two walls of God's will and His presence.*

servant and prophet of God, a leader and judge of God's people, and a man of faithful prayer.

You (and I) are to be strong so you will experience success in your undertakings. Strength comes from knowing your job assignments, which creates certain limitations. And limitations serve to sharpen your focus and channel your energy. To know what you *must* do shows you what you *can't do* (or what you must give up, put aside, or postpone). These limitations create a powerful, singular focus. Like the Colorado River carving the Grand Canyon, something magnificent comes from funneling your life between the two walls of God's will (revealed through His commands and job assignments) and His promised presence. When God's will looks impossible, the promise of His presence (and all that it includes—His power, His guidance, His wisdom, His comfort, His provision, His encouragement) strengthens you to take the first step and move forward.

3. *Be around older Christian women.* When you're in the presence of more seasoned and spiritually mature sisters in Christ, you grow. You see their strength and sense their power firsthand. Being near them enables you to watch how they handle life and people and problems. You can take note of how they think with clarity and act with wisdom. And you're able to observe what their years and experiences have taught them about God and His provision. You will receive an infusion of strength!

There are certain women that when I even stand beside them I get something—clues to their strength, their grace, their courage. I know one woman who asked her pastor's wife to be with her in the delivery room when her husband was in Iraq and her baby was born because she wanted high accountability for her behavior at that difficult time. Hence, her pastor's wife! The presence of that more mature woman brought something out in this woman, a certain stability. She was infused with the older woman's strength and trust in God.

4. *Don't listen to the world.* This may come as a shock or surprise, but your television and its daily programming usually won't help you be a strong Christian woman. Yes, there are fine Christian programs, but in general television doesn't help you focus on God and the roles He's given you as a woman after His heart. Turn on your TV and you're bombarded by the world's standards, which can create confusion and temptation. The more you hear and see, the more uncertain you may become about being a Christian woman and what you should do and not do. Why? Because you're listening to the world, which is giving and promoting false information. When you're not sure, you might become double-minded, torn about what to do. You become unstable in your ways. What you're looking for is one clear message...God's message found in His Word. This singleness of message, this focus, will give you strength. It will bring you courage for what your day—and your life—holds in store.

5. *Recite "Someone has to..." and fill in the blank.* I learned this from Edith Schaeffer's book *What Is a Family?* Throughout the book she wrote, "Someone has to" and then she filled in the blank with what she was teaching. Filling in the blank helps me stiffen my resolve and encourage myself so I'll be strong and courageous. I tell myself, *Well, someone has to do this...and it's going to be me.*

One of the things Mrs. Schaeffer mentioned in the first chapter of her book is "Someone has to make the family a career. Someone has to spend the time and make the effort to make a family happen." Who's that someone to be? If it's not the woman, the wife, the mom, who is it going to be? And the answer is probably no one. Someone has to give the time, the effort, the hard work, the sacrifice, and the planning to make a family successful. Someone has to possess the certainty that family is important (even while the world tells us that "me" is what counts). Someone has to spend the rest of her life paying the price to have a family. Mrs. Schaeffer ends chapter one by stating, "The individual families making up society have to be really worked on by someone."[3]

If "someone has to do this or do that" helps you resolve to turn your commitment to your job assignments of wife and mom up to the maximum setting and move on it, great! *Someone has to.*

6. *Study God's Word.* I *l-o-v-e* reading about the life of David in the Bible. I especially enjoy the part where he fought against Goliath, the giant (1 Samuel 17). You see, David was just a shepherd boy. He spent his days out in the fields with sheep...but he also spent them *with the Lord.* He passed the lonely hours and days of solitude by tending the animals, singing songs to God, playing his lute, and thinking on the Lord and His care, protection, provision, and promises.

> *When you're close to God, spending time in His Word, you see clearly.*

One day his father sent him to the battlefront to take food to his older brothers. When he arrived, Goliath came to the battle line and threatened God's people—again. He taunted them and put down their God. The result? The Israelite soldiers panicked and fled. But David, who had a fresh perspective because he'd spent much time focused on God, said, in essence, to the warriors, "Don't let that guy talk to you like that! Sure, he's big, but you're the army of the living God!" David was like the child who sees thing as they are and says it (remember *The Emperor and His New Clothes* story?). The shepherd boy could see what the seasoned warriors didn't see. Because he'd been close to God, he viewed things differently—and accurately.

The same is true for you! When you're close to God, spending time in His Word, you see clearly. You see a situation for what it is. You possess strength, courage, wisdom, and proper perspective. And all because you've been focused on God!

7. *Remember the women at the cross.* This is my "when all else fails" catchall prompt for gaining strength and courage. I remember the women at the cross and the tomb of Jesus. Whenever I read Mark, chapters 15 and 16, I'm always amazed that a small band of women stayed with our Lord to the very end, even when His closest disciples—the men—left! These women stood near the cross through Jesus' horrendous torture and suffering. And their devotion didn't end with His death. They followed those who carried the Lord's body to the tomb where He was placed.

And their devotion didn't end even then. They returned to their homes after the worst day of their lives and prepared for the Sabbath. They continued to serve the Lord by faithfully purchasing and mixing the burial spices for anointing His body: "When the Sabbath was past, [they] bought spices, that they might come and anoint Him" (Mark 16:1).

You and I might think, *Well, it's over. I'm going to go on with my life.* But not so these women. Very early in the morning, after the Sabbath, after all the trauma of the crucifixion and the ominous darkness on the day before, they came to the tomb where Jesus' body had been laid as the sun rose.

Our natural human tendency is to check for loopholes, to look for an excuse or reason that will get us out of having to show up or having to do something. These women left for the sepulcher not even knowing who would roll the huge stone away from the door of the tomb (verse 3). Next to this verse, I've written in my Bible, "They didn't let a little thing like a massive stone keep them from going."

I draw strength from these gallant women who endured a tumultuous day that ended with the horror of the crucifixion of their Lord and Savior. And they wanted to do all they could for Him. If I'd experienced even part of what these women went through, I might have taken two aspirin and stayed in bed for two or three days to recover from the trauma. So whenever I want to take a shortcut, pass on something important or risky, or in some way slight my family, I remember the women at the cross. These women served faithfully in the midst of extreme difficulty. May you and I be so faithful!

## *Moving Forward*

Life regularly presents us with choices. You have a choice about how and what you're going to think about and how you're going to act. You can go against Scripture and react to situations with worry, anger, sadness, or frustration...or you can bring your thoughts under control and focus them between the two rock-solid walls of God's canyon:

- God's will—"Have I not commanded you?"
- God's presence—"I am with you wherever you go."

When God asks (or commands, as He did with Joshua) you to do something that looks impossible, do it! With courage take that first step. Don't think about all that might happen. Don't worry about the road ahead. Choose to direct your thoughts between those two divine walls. When you do, your life will gain godly force. You will be strong, powerful, and gain momentum as you bravely move forward, knowing God is with you through everything. As Jesus said, "With God all things are possible" (Mark 10:27).

*He who fears God need fear nothing else, and he who fears not God needs to fear everything else.*[1]

# 7

# *Fighting Your Fears*

*Have I not commanded you?*
*Be strong and of good courage;*
*do not be afraid, nor be dismayed,*
*for the* LORD *your God is with you*
*wherever you go.*

JOSHUA 1:9

Have you felt fearful about the future? Uncertain about your abilities? Unsure of yourself? I don't know about you, but I have moments like these almost every day. As I face an impossible day, new challenges, the many chances of failure, and people who aren't always friendly or supportive, I think how much easier it might be to cancel all appointments, skip work, and choose to stay home for the day. Why even try? But God has work for me to do—important work! He has a plan that somehow, amazingly, involves me. So I wrestle with the fears and doubts that so regularly come my way and draw on God's strength.

Joshua must have felt like this when God revealed His special purpose and assignment to him. In the opening chapter of Joshua, God is speaking heart to heart with His hesitant and fearful servant. What were God's instructions? "Joshua, there's a land to conquer and a war to wage. You're a warrior, and I want you to take up My call and lead the battle."

Perhaps Joshua wondered, *How can I move forward on this fearsome, awesome command? How can I possibly take the first step?* God tells him how! He begins by commanding Joshua to look to His Word, to learn it by heart, and to do whatever He says (Joshua 1:8). On the heels of these orders comes this question from the Lord—along with more commands to "Arise, go over this Jordan...Have I not commanded you? Be strong and of good courage" (verses 2 and 9).

For nine verses we don't read any dialogue or verbal interchange between God and Joshua. No, it's all *God*—God *talking* to Joshua, *commanding* Joshua, *encouraging* Joshua, *strengthening* Joshua, *instructing* Joshua, *making and repeating promises* to Joshua. And when God spoke, Joshua listened. But he must have been afraid, because four times in this initial chapter God addresses Joshua's fears and gives him a barrage of encouragement (verses 6-7,9,18). Verse 9, however, adds two negative admonishments and a promise.

First let's look at the promise.

### *Count on God's Promise*

I've often heard that "God's work will never lack God's provision." That's exactly what God offered Joshua. Regardless of the task, challenge, impossible mission, or whether Joshua would have another person with him, at all times, no matter what was happening, wherever he was, or whatever he was facing, God promised *His presence*. God assured Joshua that He would be with him throughout the campaign of winning the land through battle—and beyond. God would be with Joshua his entire life.

> *You can count on God's strength!*

You too have God's promise to count on. *He* will be with *you* from the moment you accept His Son as Lord and Savior and throughout eternity! Wow! Like Joshua, you can step out bravely to accomplish the list of fierce and difficult actions you get to take as you live out God's will for you.

## *Pay Attention to the Don'ts*

Just in case Joshua was still a little squeamish about moving forward, God admonished him with two prohibitions:

- ❧ Do not be afraid.
- ❧ Do not be dismayed.

*"Do not be afraid"*—Fear is not reserved for the weak. Joshua was a leader of leaders and a warrior with a proven war record. Yet God spent considerable time bolstering Joshua's courage and admonishing him about the dangers of fear. God knew the future, and He knew that humans tend to worry and doubt—no matter who they are. So just in case Joshua would be facing a "superior" enemy (and he would be for sure—there were giants in the land!), and just in case he might be tempted to be afraid (and who wouldn't?), Joshua could look back on this incredible encounter with God and recall the encouragement and support God provided for setting out—and finishing!—a divine commission. And God will help you fight your fears too!

*Remember your encounter with God*—Think back on that moment, on that day when you met Jesus and surrendered your life to His leading. When Jesus came into your life, He promised to stay. He said He would never leave you and He would never forsake you (Hebrews 13:5). Do you believe Him? Faith and trust in your Savior will help you fight your fears—any fears, whether of people, or lack, or loss, or battle, or the future. Faith fights fear!

*Review God's promises*—God spent time reminding Joshua of the promises He'd made to Moses concerning the invasion of the Promised Land. God told Joshua, "Every place that the sole of your foot will tread upon I have given you, as I said to Moses" (Joshua 1:3). Then the Lord added this additional reminder, "No man shall be able to stand before you all the days of your life; as I was with Moses, so I will be with you. I will not leave you nor forsake you" (verse 5).

God has given us many great and wonderful promises concerning everything from salvation to eternal life, from the new birth to a final home in heaven, from new beginnings to spiritual maturity and great usefulness to the body of Christ. God promised Joshua His presence, and that promise still stands for us today. In fact, God has promised in His Word not to withhold any good thing from us and to give us all good things (Psalm 84:11; Romans 8:32)! So don't wait until a challenge comes and your fear begins to mount. Fight fear *before* it begins by regularly reviewing God's promises and holding them in your heart.

*Do not be dismayed.* You'll love this bit of negative instruction. God is telling Joshua not to get depressed or become cast down. Depression, often the twin sister of fear, is a major problem for people, and unfortunately it often strikes Christians. But we have an option! We can *refuse* to be dismayed. We can determine not to be depressed. We can instead make these choices:

- *Remember your Father.* You are a child of the God of the universe. You have a royal heritage. There's not one reason for you to ever be discouraged, depressed, or dismayed as a daughter of the King of kings.
- *Review God's promises,* especially this one: "His divine power has given to us *all things* that pertain to life and godliness" (2 Peter 1:3). With a promise like this, you never have to fear, doubt, or worry!

## *Strength in the Midst of Fear*

God says, *"Be strong."* What do you think of when you hear or read the word "strong"? What images enter your mind? My mind runs to weightlifters, wrestlers, fighters, and soldiers. I also think of rocks and stones, of the Granite Mountains near the place where I was born in Oklahoma. Then there's steel. And, of course, inner strength—something in the character of a person who stands in adversity, who acts and speaks up because it's the right thing to do, who moves forward toward a goal or purpose regardless of the cost or obstacles, who endures through harsh and trying times and treatment.

> *Power, force, and momentum will come as you begin to walk in God's will.*

When God told Joshua to "be strong," it was an order, something Joshua was to do. Such strength is not a fruit of the Spirit that's exhibited when walking in harmony with God (see Galatians 5:22-23). And it's not something that comes automatically with salvation through Christ. And it has nothing to do with a believer's position in Christ. No, God was commanding Joshua to "be strong," to strengthen himself, to encourage himself, to harden himself, and to behave valiantly.

God is telling Joshua that he is to move out in battle and conquer the land on the other side of the Jordan River...whether he wants to or not, whether he feels like doing it or not, whether he thinks he can win or not, whether he's up for it or not. Joshua is basically told "Just do it!" He's not to be feeble, fragile, or frightened about this command. He's to be strong and move forward.

And you and I have to do the same. When everything in us chafes or shies away from doing what's in front of us that must be done or endured or finished, we have to stand up, buck up, look up, and just do it. We have to strengthen ourselves, encourage ourselves, harden ourselves, and behave valiantly. We have to *step up* to the challenge, stare it in the face, and then boldly *step into* it—into the waters of the Jordan, if you will—before we can cross it and conquer it.

Like the Colorado River forming the Grand Canyon, as we begin to move forward between the two massive walls of God's will on one side and His presence on the other, we'll discover sufficient strength for the task. Power, force, and momentum will come as we begin to walk—or even tiptoe!—ahead...no matter what. As F.B. Meyer so eloquently writes,

> Each square mile of [the Promised Land] had to be claimed from the hand of the people that possessed it. "The sole of the foot" had to be put down to claim and take. The cities were theirs, but they must enter them; the houses which they had not built were theirs, but they must inhabit them. The cornfields in the rich vales, and vineyards on the terraced slopes were theirs, but they must possess them. [God's blessings] are only ours as we avail ourselves of them. Hence the need to "be strong and very courageous."

## *What's in Front of You?*

Are you staring into a seemingly impossible day? As I'm writing, it's winter. And my daughter Katherine lives in New York where winters are brutal. Yesterday she stepped into what she thought would be a "normal" day. She dropped two of her children off at school and returned home to a full Monday. (Ho hum. So what's new?) She went downstairs to the basement laundry room to begin her many loads of laundry...only to find that a pipe had broken and the floor was completely flooded. Wondering about the attached duplex next door that was vacant and her husband had almost finished remodeling, she ran into the duplex...to discover the basement there was also flooded, as well as the kitchen above it from a second broken pipe.

Katherine went into action. She called her husband for advice, called their insurance agent, and started into her first five hours of mopping, bailing water, and moving possessions.

Today (Day 2) the plumber came and found yet another leak in Katherine's upstairs master bedroom, which had flooded the dry garage where she and her husband had moved their furniture. All of Paul's hard work of painting, tiling, and putting down hardwood floors is ruined in both sides of their home, as well as much of their furniture and possessions.

I'm so Christian proud of my daughter! The emails she sent shared her shock, her woes, her challenges, the details of the catastrophe...but they also share her "roll up your sleeves attitude" as she moved into action. And her tales were sprinkled throughout with thanksgiving to God that the flooding wasn't worse, that it wasn't a horrendous tragedy, that, as her young children said, "It's OK, Mom. It's only stuff."

Katherine strengthened herself for her battle, her ordeal, her surprise Black Monday, her almost literal Jordan River. I haven't asked her, but there may have been tears—after all, it was her *home.* But she was strong. She tackled the problem. Like Joshua, Katherine followed God's instructions to *be strong* when facing giants...and giant, distressing situations. She stepped into God's will for her days of fighting disaster.

### *Facing Your Giants*

Maybe my daughter Kath's situation seems somewhat trivial and "daily" compared to what's in front of you today. But every problem—every giant!—and all trouble is to be confronted in the same way and with the same decisiveness, strength, and grace that only comes from God. What's in front of each of us is God's will for us this minute and this day. We have our own personal challenges. Our Jordans. And we're to arise and go through them and over to the other side.

Perhaps you're facing a frightening life or death situation for yourself or a loved one. I know this scenario better than I'd like. I have a daughter who recently had a malignant lung tumor removed and faced the terrors that cancer can mean. I have a sister-in-law who's facing chemotherapy for her newly diagnosed cancer. I have a brother who died recently from cancer after bravely enduring many treatments. And I've already lost a sister-in-law to this disease.

The list of fearful, distressing challenges we encounter goes on and on. They extend way beyond ruined property, catastrophes, and cancer. Susanna Wesley (mother of John and Charles Wesley) had 19 children, 10 of whom died before they were two years old and five who died within the space of four years. And one of her daughters was born crippled in body.

Fanny Crosby, one of God's songbirds and the writer of more than 8,000 hymns, woke up every day of her 95-year-life blind. Christian missionaries John and Betty Stam woke up one morning and walked the road to martyrdom by decapitation. Dale Evans Rogers woke up every day knowing her little daughter's disease would cause her death before she was ten. Catherine Marshall sat beside her newborn granddaughter's tube ridden body for the six weeks she lived and painstakingly, prayerfully, and powerfully crossed through each day.

### *Victory Is Yours!*

But your life isn't about failures. Joshua 1:9 is about victory! It's about facing your fears and your giants, trusting God, crossing your rivers, and conquering the unknown without getting discouraged or becoming dismayed. That's what Joshua did because that's what he was commanded by God to do next.

And how is victory won? And what gives us the ability to think straight and make good decisions under duress? To keep a clear head and resist the temptation to give in to sorrow or depression? And just where are we supposed to obtain the energy and courage needed to even take a deep breath and take the first step into God's will and our present challenge?

Power, valor, and victory come as you and I obediently press on by faith between the two walls erected on each side of us by God, as noted in Joshua 1:9. You will be able to follow God with all your heart, face your fears and demands, and fight on to gain the victory when you count on:

- God's will—*"Have I not commanded you?"*
- God's presence—*The Lord your God is with you wherever you go.*

God gives the orders, and God goes with us! He reveals His will to us and walks with us and strengthens us as we do His will. And our part? "Be strong and of good courage; do not be afraid, nor be dismayed, for the Lord your God is with you wherever you go" (Joshua 1:9). "Arise, go over this Jordan" (verse 2). These instructions and truths infuse us with strength...strength to move forward, strength to keep moving forward, and strength to triumph over all odds and live out God's plan.

## *Moving Forward*

Is your courage a little thin these days? Do you feel overwhelmed or like you're bordering on being overwhelmed by tough issues and demanding responsibilities? Are your fears getting the best of you? Bolster your nerve and fight your fears by remembering these fundamentals:

- *Prayer dispels fear and doubt.* The Bible says you're not to be double-minded, for the woman who doubts is unstable in all her ways (James 1:6-8). So pray, says verse 5! There's phenomenal, unexplainable strength in knowing God's will. It emboldens you to follow Him with power and bravery. Search the Bible for God's direction and ask for it through prayer. And once you find it, move out! No wondering. No doubts. No fears. And no wishing your life was different. Just do God's will!

- *Focusing on the finish line diminishes fear.* As a Christian, you know you'll spend eternity with God. There will be less fear in following God when you keep your eyes on that end—the finish line of heaven. There will be little or no waffling and wavering when you keep the promise of life forever with Jesus fresh and alive. No matter what happens along the way to doing God's will and fulfilling His plan, you know you'll experience fullness of joy and pleasures forevermore (Psalm 16:11).
- *Forward momentum forces fear aside.* Proceeding forward pushes fear aside. Like the snowball that rolls down an incline, you gain speed, mass, and momentum as you step out and do what God asks. Soon you'll discover your fears have been left behind.

When you pray, focus on your future and boldly advance. You are following hard after God with all your heart (Psalm 63:8).

*Fear not, for I am with you;*
*Be not dismayed, for I am your God.*
*I will strengthen you, yes, I will help you,*
*I will uphold you with*
*My righteous right hand.*

Isaiah 41:10

8

# *Counting on the Presence of God*

*Have I not commanded you?*
*Be strong and of good courage;*
*do not be afraid, nor be dismayed,*
*for the* Lord *your God is with you*
*wherever you go.*

Joshua 1:9

I love living in the sparsely populated backwoods of Western Washington State. Jim and I are six miles from the nearest (and only) stop sign in town. Most of our handful of neighbors are shielded from our sight by massive cedar, fir, and pine trees. At night all we can hear is the sound of "nothing." In fact—and this may be hard to believe—it's so quiet we have trouble sleeping without the aid of a sound machine. Yes, this tranquil part of God's earth is a great place for a writer. I enjoy the solitude...as long as I have my Jim by my side. Now that I think about it, maybe I'm not such a solitary person after all!

Few people in this world enjoy being alone...at least for extended periods of time. And that's biblical. God created us to be social beings. From the beginning of recorded time He knew humans needed companionship. God said, "It is not good for the man to be alone; I will make a helper suitable for him" (Genesis 2:18 NIV). God created Eve for Adam, to be his companion, and the two became the first married couple. And if you're not married, God has given you friends and family for companionship. You also have your church family who will come alongside you in the good times as well as the bad.

Companionship is available. But when God said, "It is not good for the man to be alone," He could just as easily have been speaking of the spiritual side of companionship.

## *The God Who Is There*

Two favorite books Jim and I enjoyed together were *The God Who Is There* and *He Is There and He Is Not Silent,* written by the late Francis Schaeffer. These books are a layperson's guide on the subject of God and how we can know Him. A prominent theme is God's omnipresence, meaning God is present everywhere and always. He's the creator and sustainer of the universe. The entire Bible is infused with hundreds of verses speaking of God's presence. The psalmist rhetorically asks, "Where can I go from Your Spirit? Or where can I flee from Your presence?" He then spends the next five verses affirming the short answer—*nowhere!* Whether it is the farthest reaches of the earth or the depths of the sea or the darkest of nights, God is present (Psalm 139:7-12).

## *The God Who Is Not Silent*

For Joshua, God's promise of His presence was great news. The warrior was about to embark on the greatest battle of his life. Humanly speaking, the odds were decidedly against him. His ill-trained army consisted of the children of former slaves—no match for the fortified cities and trained armies found in Canaan. Unless God was with him, Joshua knew there was no hope. So when Joshua heard God say, "The Lord your God is with you wherever you go" (Joshua 1:9), you know Joshua's confidence level rose.

What does God's presence look like and what did Joshua experience as he carried out God's orders to cross the Jordan and conquer the land? Check it out!

- ✓ God affirmed His power to Rahab, a harlot who lived in Jericho, so she would risk her life to protect Joshua's two spies and send them on their way back to him after they spied out Jericho (Joshua 2).
- ✓ God miraculously parted the Jordan River at flood stage so Joshua's army could cross on dry ground (Joshua 3:14-17).
- ✓ God—again miraculously—brought the walls of the great fortified city of Jericho tumbling down with only the blowing of trumpets and the shouts of Joshua's men after seven days of the army simply walking around the city (Joshua 6).
- ✓ God, in yet another miracle, cast down large hailstones during one battle that killed more of the enemy than those who died in battle (Joshua 10:11).
- ✓ God, in a second miracle during the same battle with the hail, made the sun stand still to protect Joshua against the Amorites so his army could rout out the enemy (Joshua 10:12-14).
- ✓ God delivered a large coalition of the kings of Northern Canaan into Joshua's hands, which effectively divided the land in half, making conquest much easier (Joshua 11:6-8).

For Joshua, God's presence was mightily visible in His active involvement in the warrior's life and on his missions. God was present…and He was definitely not silent! The bottom line of God's presence for Joshua was success—"Joshua took the whole land, according to all that the LORD had said to Moses" (Joshua 11:23).

The question for us today? Is this the same God who's at work in our lives?

## *What About God's Presence in Your Life?*

As you're reading along, are you thinking, *But that's the Old Testament and that was Joshua. That was a special situation in the life of a special person. God doesn't work that way today.* True, God isn't actively holding back rivers, casting down large hail on your enemies, or bringing down the walls of fortified cities, but that doesn't mean He couldn't! And that doesn't mean He isn't present and just as active in your life. In fact, this is where biblical truth gets really exciting!

*God's presence is not limited*—For many people, and maybe even you, God's presence is viewed as being limited to, or at least particularly present in, a building. God is reverently portrayed and symbolized in beautiful stained-glass scenes, burning candles, and worshipful organ music. We all appreciate these sensual prompts for worship. It's true that these accessories contribute to a *sense* of God's presence. But is God limited to a building? This was the same question asked of Jesus by a woman at a well over 2,000 years ago. Listen in on a most incredible conversation between a seeking heart and the Lord Jesus Christ, God in flesh:

> "Our fathers worshiped on this mountain [Samaria], and you Jews say that in Jerusalem [the site of the Jewish Temple] is the place where one ought to worship."
>
> Jesus said to her, "Woman, believe Me, the hour is coming when you will neither on this mountain, nor in Jerusalem, worship the Father...But the hour is coming, and now is, when the true worshipers will worship the Father in spirit and truth...God is spirit, and those who worship Him must worship in spirit and truth" (John 4:20-21,23-24)

"God is spirit." So God is without limits and can be worshiped and communicated with anywhere and anytime. What a wonderful reality! The God of the Universe is with you *right now* wherever you are! He is personally interested in any and every one of your deepest sorrows and hurts, your greatest opportunities, and the decisions you must make. Count on it!

*God's presence is spiritual*—God's presence in Joshua's life was very obvious because God spoke to him and performed miracle after miracle. But God also gave Joshua "the spirit of wisdom" (Deuteronomy 34:9). God's Spirit came *upon* Joshua, but God didn't reside *in* Joshua. That's the main difference between Joshua and believers today.

*What an amazing miracle—the abiding presence of God in your life...for all of your life!*

Jesus said the Father will "give you another Helper, that He may abide with you forever—the Spirit of truth" (John 14:16-17). Those who know and love Jesus are given the Holy Spirit to be *with* and *in* them for as long as they are physically alive. So for you as a Christian, God's presence takes on an even deeper significance. What an amazing miracle—the abiding presence of God *in* your life... for all of your life!

*God's presence is real*—How can you or I explain the presence of God? Well, you can see His handiwork in creation: "For since the creation of the world His invisible attributes are clearly seen, being understood by the things that are made, even His eternal power" (Romans 1:20; see also Psalm 19:1). You can't see the Spirit of God, but what you do have is Jesus' word that He is present, which must be believed by faith. You also have the outworking of His presence in your life—the fruit of the Spirit: love, joy, peace, longsuffering, kindness, goodness, faithfulness, gentleness, self-control (Galatians 5:22-23). Let me explain with two different situations in my life.

> On one rare occasion I was traveling alone. My flight was rerouted due to a blizzard. The weather was awful! It was one of those stranded-in-an-airport-all-night scenarios. There wasn't any way to let Jim know what was happening or what might happen. I had that sinking feeling of being utterly alone. Then I remembered that I wasn't. I prayed, "God, not one of my loved ones in this whole world knows where I am. But *You* do!" The promise of God's presence reassured me that I wasn't lost in space, and I experienced an amazing sense of peace knowing God was with me. God's peace came when I remembered the truth of His presence.
>
> The other time was when I was having major surgery. As the staff wheeled me into the operating room, and Jim was left behind in the waiting room. I lay on the gurney helpless and sedated. I prayed, "Lord, yea, though I may be walking through the valley of the shadow of death [I didn't know what the surgeon might find], yea, though I may be entering the unknown, and yea, though I'm being put under with anesthesia, You are with me!" And do you know what? God was…and He is! We never have to ask for His presence. We only need to remember the fact and reality of it.

In spite of what some might say about God, you and I can know one thing absolutely, and it's the same thing Joshua and the saints through the ages knew: God is with us wherever we go…forever! And that gives us courage day by day.

*God's presence is a good thing*—God's presence was a good thing for Joshua, and it should be seen as a great thing for Christians today. But sadly, many believers aren't that excited about knowing God is everywhere all the time. Why? The answer's found in a single, small word: "sin." Like Adam and Eve who hid themselves from the presence of the Lord God after disobeying Him (Genesis 3:8), our sin alters our relationship with God. When we live in sin and hang on to it, we usually look for ways to hide our sins *and* ourselves from Him or pretend He isn't here.

Think with me for a minute. Can you remember when God wasn't in your life, before you were His child? Do you recall what an awful time that was? How desperate and hopeless life seemed to be? I sure can, and I don't want my close relationship and life with God to be jeopardized in any way. And I'm sure you don't either!

Being confident of God's presence is wonderful. Whenever you sense your relationship with God growing a little distant, do your part to close the gap. Search your heart. Confess any and all sin to God (1 John 1:9), and then you'll again revel in the joy of full communion with God. That's what David wrote about after his heartfelt confession concerning his sin of adultery with Bathsheba: "Blessed is he whose transgression is forgiven, whose sin is covered...I said, 'I will confess my transgressions to the LORD,' and You forgave the iniquity of my sin" (Psalm 32:1,5).

*God's presence is a comfort*—I'm sure you realize you live in a hostile world. Pain and suffering are facts of life. And maybe, like me, you wish you could avoid as much as possible of that pain, grief, loss, sorrow, and other difficulties. But God comes to your aid!

> The righteous cry out, and the LORD hears, and delivers them out of all their troubles. The LORD is near to those who have a broken heart, and saves such as have a contrite spirit. Many are the afflictions of the righteous, but the LORD delivers him out of them all (Psalm 34:17-19).

*God's presence is empowering*—This marvelous fact brings us back to following God with all your heart. God's presence was empowering for Joshua. Knowing God was with him enabled the warrior to do great and mighty deeds. And it's no different for you.

With God, you can do—and endure—all things through Christ who strengthens you (Philippians 4:13).

You also have God's ever-present grace, which is sufficient for anything you will ever face, no matter how big or how bad. As Jesus told Paul regarding his suffering, "My grace is sufficient for you" (2 Corinthians 12:9).

The Holy Spirit infuses you with His power, giving you wisdom, patience, faithfulness. There's no need to fear serving others and stepping out into ministry! (And believe me, it can feel scary out there!) No, the Holy Spirit gives you "spiritual gifts" to use in ministry to the body of Christ (1 Corinthians 12:1-11).

*When difficulties strike, don't get upset. Instead, thank God for His presence and together forge ahead in victory.*

As we end this chapter on God's promise of His presence, I pray this knowledge is and will be a source of strength and courage for you. Here's one more thought to file away: Sometimes God chooses to deliver you from your problems, and at other times He will give you the strength to endure them. In either case, you can rest assured His comforting presence is with you, and He will see you through.

When difficulties strike (and strike they will), you don't have to get upset or frustrated. Instead, thank God for His presence, and then together—you and He—forge on ahead in victory. Victory is yours when God's in your corner!

## *Moving Forward*

Have you thought much about the constant and abiding presence of God in *your* home, *your* life, *your* difficulties, and *your* opportunities? The God of the universe is with you whether you acknowledge Him or not. So why not start actively practicing the presence of God? Get ready for a huge difference in your life and in your faith if you do. How can you start moving forward with more awareness of Him?

*Acknowledge God's presence in your life.* With every activity, acknowledge God's presence verbally or in silent prayer. When you get up in the morning, thank God for your life, for another day to serve Him, live for Him, and walk with Him through whatever comes your way. He's with you through your surprises, catastrophes, and the never-ending, routine dailies that sometime seem to drag on and not make much difference. When you get into your car, a bus, a taxi, a boat or ship, or on an airplane, stop and affirm God's presence and allow Him to comfort you as you travel. When you pray before your meals, pause a little longer and bask in His provision *and* His presence. The more you are aware of His presence, the more your relationship with Him will take on greater significance.

Count on His presence as you go about your day, no matter what pops up along the way. The harder your tasks or more terrifying your challenges, factor in your heavenly Father's omnipresence. He's right there with you, ready and able to comfort, encourage, strengthen, and supply you with His divine wisdom, grace, and power.

*Acknowledge God's presence to others.* You honor God and give Him glory when you make His presence known to others. Your awareness of Him and dependency on Him is not something to be ashamed of or kept hidden. If you knew a celebrity or a great personality, you'd be proud of your friendship and want everyone to know. Well, who is greater than God? And He's here with you always! As you acknowledge Him verbally to others—beginning with your family!—you're announcing to everyone around you that you have a personal relationship with God and saying they can too. As the psalmist exclaimed, "Let the redeemed of the LORD say so" (Psalm 107:2).

# Section 3

# *Becoming an Exceptional Woman*

*Don't let the world around you*
*squeeze you into its own mould,*
*but let God re-mould your minds*
*from within, so that you may prove*
*in practice that the plan of God for you*
*is good, meets all his demands, and*
*moves towards the goal of true maturity.*

Romans 12:2 Phillips

# 9

# *Living Above the Norm*

*Do not be conformed to this world,*
*but be transformed by the renewing of your mind,*
*that you may prove what is that good and*
*acceptable and perfect will of God.*

ROMANS 12:2

Well, my conference near the Grand Canyon is over. It was a wonderful time! Afterward, on the way back to the Phoenix airport, the woman driving Jim and me told us about a carload of women who attended the retreat several years earlier and missed a crucial freeway split on their way home. It was a divide where the exit to the left went to Phoenix, Arizona, and the one to the right went to Los Angeles, California. These dear ladies were having such a good time discussing their time at the retreat...that they ended up in California! Imagine their shock when they read the "Welcome to California" sign at the state border!

How about you? Have you missed some turns, some forks in the road driving down a freeway...or in life?

## *The Fork in the Road*

There's a point in any and every journey where a decision has to be made: "Which way do I go?" Hopefully you make the decision before you speed past the opportunity to go in the direction you need or want to go. There's nothing worse than having to get off a road, figure out how to backtrack, turn around, and get back on the highway so you can make the right choice this time.

The same is true in your life as a believer. For a Christian, a priority is, "How can I know God's will? How can I be in God's will? Which choices will keep me on the path of God's will?" These questions are essential to ask and answer if you—and me too!—want to follow God with all your heart. The desire to follow Him and live in His will sets you apart from the normal life and puts you into an extraordinary one.

I have good news! God gives you His formula for finding, following, and living His will. It's found in Romans 12:1-2. For a clearer understanding of these two verses (especially verse 2) consider that in Romans, chapters 1–11, the apostle Paul lays down what has been referred to as "The Gospel According to Paul." He writes at length about the doctrinal foundation of Christianity. Then, in chapter 12, Paul turns to the practical issues and concerns of everyday life. First he appeals to us in verse 1:

> I beseech you therefore, brethren, by the mercies of God, that you present your bodies a living sacrifice, holy, acceptable to God, which is your reasonable service.

We're exhorted to offer our *bodies* to God, to set them apart and dedicate them to God's service and righteous living (see also 1 Corinthians 6:13). That's key to following God and being useful to Him. Then in verse 2, Paul tells us to offer our *minds* to God:

> Do not be conformed to this world, but be transformed by the renewing of your mind, that you may prove what is that good and acceptable and perfect will of God.

## *Be on Your Guard*

Once you and I offer ourselves completely to God—our bodies and our minds—a dramatic change occurs in our relationship with the world. Christianity is a calling *away* from worldliness. Christ delivers believers "*from* this present evil age" (Galatians 1:4). If we are in Christ, the Bible says we are to behave as "obedient children, *not* conforming yourselves to the former lusts" (1 Peter 1:14).

Every day, maybe even every minute, you will be tempted and pressured to conform to the world, to live as an unbeliever. But don't give in to the pressures of worldliness. Instead, "gird up the loins of your mind, be sober, and rest your hope fully upon the grace [offered by Jesus]" (verse 13). Live *for* God and live His way.

An exceptional woman—you!—follows the teachings in verses 1 and 2 of Romans 12. You give your body and soul, mind and heart to God for His use and service. And you're on the lookout for any forks along the road of life so you can prayerfully consider your decisions. As you understand more and more how extraordinary you are, you'll delight in rejecting worldly behavior and devoting the minutes and hours and days of your life to making wise decisions regarding your behavior and choices.

## *Ordinary or Extraordinary?*

No one wants to be ordinary or to lead a hum-drum, ho-hum life. After all, you have the power of Christ in you and an exciting purpose for your life and your every day. Oh sure, you desire order and peace. And you're instructed to look for ways to lead a tranquil, peaceful life (1 Timothy 2:2; 1 Thessalonians 4:11). But that doesn't mean boredom! And inactivity is not God's way.

> *Living life based on the truths in the Bible makes you a unique woman!*

Romans 12:2 shows us what being extraordinary means. It's refusing to think and behave as those in the world do. When we do this—when we reason and act differently—we stand out from all that is common. By firmly founding our minds on the attitudes and truths consistent with new life in Christ, we transcend what is average. In fact, there's nothing average about us at all because we're extraordinary!

Thinking and living based on the truths in the Bible will create a unique woman—you again!—who towers above the norm. When you think on God's Word, you will have your mind transformed and find God's will—His "good and acceptable and perfect will." You'll be able to *discern* God's will, *perform* His will, and *live* His will. And you'll have the added benefit of experiencing and living that which is good and well-pleasing and perfect in His eyes for you! This, my friend, sets you apart from all that is ordinary.

*You* are exceptional. Think about it! Christ lives in you. That should—and does!—make a huge difference in your life. That sets you light years above this world! You're markedly unique! When you came to Christ—became a believer in Him—you were transformed on the inside. But now you make that transformation real to yourself and others by letting it show on the outside. And that's done by refusing to live according to the customs of the world.

Did you notice the words "do not be" in Romans 12:2? This is a command from God. It's not a suggestion. And it's not a little bit of good advice or a tip. This is also not an excerpt from a "Dear Abby" column. No, this is *God* speaking. He's telling you:

- Do not fashion yourself after the world.
- Do not configure yourself to match that of the world.
- Do not live according to the fashions of the times.
- Do not adopt the customs that the world has.
- Do not imitate the way people live in the world.

If you're doing any of these, you're instructed to stop immediately and, instead, renew and refresh your thinking. One scholar translates this part of Romans 12:12 to read, "Do not shape your lives to meet the fleeting fashions of this world." Another adds an extra descriptive word—"this *evil* world."

Now I ask you, Why would any woman with a pure, holy God living inside her heart and soul want to fashion herself after "this evil world"? "Fashioning" means to be poured into a mold, to allow something to shape your appearance. This makes me think about bread dough. I'm sure you know the process for bread making. First you mix up a batch of dough. Then you put it into any shaped pan or mold it into any shape you desire. You get to decide! You can shape your dough into little clover-leaf dinner rolls, or breadsticks, or a loaf.

When it comes to people, to you and me, we're not to let the world knead and form us like bread dough, pressing and working us into a mold.

I once saw an interview with Dr. W.A. Criswell, who at the time was the pastor of First Baptist Church in Dallas, Texas. The interview was focused on his book *Standing on the Promises*. This giant of a Christian almost cried while talking about how saddened he was to see that people could no longer distinguish a Christian from a non-Christian. He was on the verge of tears because Christians have conformed so much to the world. In fact, he believed we have brought the world into the church. He mentioned several times that he thought churches ought to quit entertaining their people and call them to holiness instead. Here was a godly man echoing God's call to Christians to transform and renew their thinking...to rethink their standards, principles, priorities, and goals...which would transform their way of living.

### *God's Roll Call of Exceptional Women*

One of my passions has been the study of the women of the Bible. God has preserved their amazing stories, their trials and triumphs, their sorrows and joys, their weaknesses and strengths, along with their contributions, for you and me in His Word. They provide inspiration, instruction, and encouragement for me on a daily basis. As I face situation after situation, I always think back to one of the women in Scripture who encountered something similar and draw a principle from her life to guide me. Her experience and wisdom help me make the right choices—the godly choices—at every opportunity, at every vital fork in the road. When I fail in my endeavor, she gives me hope. When my vision dims, she restores it. When I start to give up, she strengthens me through her great faith in God and her heart to follow Him wholeheartedly.

Here are several of the gallant women in Scripture who are described as exceptional. These women did not allow the world to conform them to its standards.

- Regarding Ruth, Boaz reported, "All the people of my town know that you are a virtuous woman" (Ruth 3:11).
- Regarding God's ideal woman—the Proverbs 31 woman—she's introduced as "a virtuous wife" and praised as one who excels all others (Proverbs 31:10 and 29).
- Regarding Mary, the mother of Jesus, God's angel greeted her by saying, "Rejoice, highly favored one, the Lord is with you; blessed are you among women!" (Luke 1:28).
- Regarding Elizabeth, she is described as "righteous before God, walking in all the commandments and ordinances of the Lord blameless" (Luke 1:6), despite the fact that her life was not perfect. She was barren, had no child, and was past the age of childbearing.

- Regarding Sarah, one of three women mentioned in God's photo album of extraordinary giants of faith in Hebrews 11:11, God records, "By faith Sarah herself also received strength to conceive seed, and she bore a child when she was past the age, because she judged Him faithful who had promised."

Amazingly, you and I have everything we need to be as remarkable as these biblical women. With God's help, we can avoid conforming to this world and follow our Lord with all our hearts. To do this we need to actively think on and recall—and count on—this fact, truth, and promise: God, in His divine power, has already given to us all things that pertain to life and godliness (2 Peter 1:3). We already possess all the makings for exceptional living.

### *Becoming an Exceptional Woman*

Do you want to stand out and live as an outstanding, exceptional, unique, uncommon, remarkable, extraordinary, nonconforming woman? Here are a few important steps.

*Guard your intake*—Feed your mind first and foremost on God's instructions. Once you know the truth and what *God* thinks about every facet of your life, you can act, think, respond, and make choices accordingly. You'll be able to make the right choices at the forks in your road. You'll be set apart from the world—"sanctified"—by the Word of God (John 17:17). Exceptional!

*Select your friends carefully.* This is a big "be careful" area. When it comes to choosing your friends, remember there are basically three kinds. The first group are those who pull you up to a higher level of Christianity, who move you closer toward God and His standards. This group includes mentors, counselors, teachers, and role models.

The next group are those who pull you along. These are like-minded peers who encourage your spiritual growth and walk with God. You're headed for the same places—greater obedience, greater growth, greater service to God and His people, and eventually to heaven and eternal life. You uplift each other along the way.

The third category is made up of acquaintances who pull you down—who encourage you in the wrong direction, pressure you to make bad choices, make fun of your standards. Yes, you love them, pray for them, serve them, and witness to them, but they are not your close friends. As the wise father in Proverbs, chapter 1, warned, "My son, if sinners entice you, do not consent. If they say, 'Come with us' [to do such and such]...do not walk in the way with them, keep your foot from their path; for their feet run to evil" (verses 10 and 15-16). In this plain language, he's instructing us as well! Don't listen to such people or copy their ways. And certainly don't follow them down their paths.

*Spend your time on what really matters.* God tells us to use our time "not as fools but as wise, redeeming the time, because the days are evil. Therefore do not be unwise, but understand what the will of the Lord is" (Ephesians 5:15-17). This means take great care in how you live. Live responsibly and wisely. Make the most of every minute by making the best use of your time. You can't afford to be reckless with your days and hours, to make poor choices about how you spend time. Your time is your life, and you're on assignment from God. You're a woman with a purpose. You were saved to serve. You are God's workmanship, created in Christ for good works (Ephesians 2:10). Seek to use your golden, God-given minutes on what really matters, not on worldly pursuits and purposes. An exceptional woman taught me this principle: "You can never kill time without injuring eternity." Being sold out to Christ most definitely affects your use of time.

*Watch what you wear.* When we realize how much God's Word has to say about His standards in this everyday area of life, we sense its importance. It may seem like a little thing, but it's a very real way we can follow God. Think about these references and let them guide your clothing choices (and your daughters' too). Christian women are to wear what is "modest" and "proper for women professing godliness, with good works" (1 Timothy 2:9-10). In other words, wear what is appropriate, moderate, and shows self-restraint.

## *Moving Forward*

When I think of standing out and living beyond the norm, I have to laugh as I remember an article I once saw in the *Los Angeles Times* business section about an award-winning commercial. The ad pictured a workroom filled with individual work booths. Because of the height of the booths, all you can see in the ad is the very top of each person's head. One head rose more than a foot above all the rest. It belonged to Kareem Abdul-Jabbar, the famous seven-foot-two former center of the Los Angeles Lakers basketball team. In the ad he's the only one in the hundred-plus booths using an Apple computer... and that made him different, setting him apart.

> *At the fork in every road, choose the road that brings you nearer to God.*

This is what God wants for you as a Christian woman. He wants you—His woman!—to be extraordinary, to tower above others, to stand out, to be above and beyond the norm. He wants you to be different, to be other-worldly. Christ in you makes you exceptional, and your thinking and behavior is to mirror your position. You're not to be like those in the world, "conformed" to the world, but you're to be special, a living, walking ambassador and advertisement for Christ.

At the fork in every road, choose the road that brings you nearer to God.

*It is not our objective to find out*
*just how much like*
*the world we can become*
*yet still maintain our distinctives.*
*Refusing to conform to this*
*world's values must go*
*even deeper than the level of*
*behavior and customs—*
*it must be firmly planted in our minds.*[1]

# 10

# *Making a Difference*

*Do not be conformed to this world,*
*but be transformed by the renewing of your mind,*
*that you may prove what is that good and*
*acceptable and perfect will of God.*

ROMANS 12:2

Butterflies...who doesn't love these delightful creatures and marvel at their exquisite beauty? In fact, you could marvel for weeks, months, and even years because there are 15,000 to 20,000 species worldwide. And did you know that many butterflies migrate over long distances? Particularly famous are the migrations of the monarch butterflies. They migrate from Mexico to North America, a distance of about 2750 miles. And some monarchs make transatlantic journeys! For looking so fragile, these delicate butterflies are truly amazing insects. But to achieve the beauty we so admire, these unique creatures go through metamorphosis.

## *A Remarkable Change*

Maybe you remember studying "metamorphosis" in an elementary science class. The butterfly starts out life as a caterpillar. The caterpillar is completely "transformed"—metamorphosed—from the inside out while in a chrysalis, the butterfly's version of a cocoon.

The same is true of you and me when we believe and trust in

Christ. We are metamorphosed! The original root of "transform" comes from the Greek language and is used in three different passages in the New Testament. One of its uses occurs in Romans 12:2: "Do not be conformed to this world, but be *transformed*." We're not to be influenced to blend into the world system. Instead, we're to be changed through Christ into creatures that fly like beautiful butterflies. Christ changes us on the inside when we are given new life in Him. "If anyone is in Christ, he is a new creation" (2 Corinthians 5:17). With the help of God's abundant grace, we need to renew our minds so that our lives are transformed externally as well, for others to see.

### *Living in the World*

Just think about it. Why be a caterpillar when you can be a butterfly? Why live a boring life when you can dazzle? Why be like unbelievers who are lost, confused, and dead in their sins, when you can live differently—in Christlikeness and confident strength? Why be ordinary when you can be different...and a difference-maker? There's one little problem with fulfilling these wonderful desires—the world. The very place where we want to make a difference is the very place where we struggle. And struggle we should. Why? Because...

- the world is presently under the control of Satan (1 John 5:19).
- the world hates Jesus because He testifies that its works are evil (John 7:7).
- the world hates you because you are Jesus' disciple (John 15:18-19).
- the world sees salvation through Christ as foolishness (1 Corinthians 1:21,27-28).

A common Christian saying drawn from John 17:15-16 that's always running through my mind says, "We are in the world but not of the world." Since we walk a fine line by being heaven bound yet having to live on earth, God provides guidelines for us regarding our relationship with the world in which we must live.

*We're to be salt* (Matthew 5:13). We're meant to have a positive influence on the world, to be to unbelievers what salt is to the food we eat. What's true of any seasoning is true of us. If a seasoning has no flavor, it has no value, appeal, or effect. And if we make no effort to live pure lives and witness to the world, we have failed in one of God's purposes for us—to cause others to desire to know God's Son. If we're too much like the world, we're worthless as "seasoning."

*We're to be light* (Matthew 5:14). Can you hide a city that's lit up and sitting on top of a hill? No! Its lights can be seen for miles as a beacon to the lost or weary traveler who needs to find a safe place to lodge for the night. Likewise we're to shine with the reflection of Christ, a radiance that emanates from the presence of Christ within our hearts. Like a glowing bride who lights up everyone around her because of her love for her groom, our love for Jesus is meant to be seen by all. However, often we hide our light by:

- being silent when we should speak
- being followers when we should lead
- being afraid to show the light
- permitting sin to dim our light
- refusing to share the light with others
- disregarding the needs of others

If we live for Christ, we'll shine like city lights on a hill, a witness of the presence and love of Christ in us, showing others the way to Him. God desires that we be beacons of truth in a dark and needy world!

*We're to make a difference* (John 17:6-18). In His prayer before going to the cross, Jesus didn't ask our heavenly Father to take believers *out* of the world. No, instead He prayed for God's protection as He left us *in* the world and sent us *into* the world (verse 18). Christ wants us to make a difference in the world where we live! The challenge is great because the world shuns Christians because our values are incompatible with its own. Because we, as Christ's followers, don't cooperate with the world by joining in its sin, people in the world see the difference and understand their immorality. Also, the world follows Satan's agenda, and Satan is the avowed enemy of Jesus and His people.

We are Jesus' ambassadors to the world. We are His witnesses to the ends of the earth. As the apostle Paul marveled, "How shall they believe in Him of whom they have not heard? And how shall they hear without a preacher?...How beautiful are the feet of those who preach the gospel of peace, who bring glad tidings of good things!" (Romans 10:14-15).

One of our job assignments is to live a holy life and share the gospel of Christ so that others will know of Him. One of God's jobs is to enable and protect us while we live righteously and share the truth with unbelievers. It is also His job to draw the hearts of men and women to Him. Our greatest challenge, then, is to live in the world and not be influenced by it. So how is our mission of witnessing to unbelievers to be accomplished? By transformation!

## *Let Transformation Begin!*

What I should actually say is "Let transformation continue!" In Romans 12:2, Paul informs us that a beautiful transformation began in our hearts the second we believed in and received Christ as Savior (see also 2 Corinthians 5:17). But Paul doesn't stop there. He lets us know that the transformation must also proceed to the *mind,* where thoughts and deeds are born.

A key to really living the Christian life is adding activities that renew your mind. "The renewing of your mind" involves a brand-new way of thinking. It indicates a mind that desires to be conformed to God and His ways instead of those of the world. No Christian can be truly transformed without renewing his or her mind.

An exceptional woman is a new being. She's one in whom God dwells. This can only mean one thing—old things have to go, including the old ways of doing things. Let's look at some areas of daily life that we need to deal with so we can grow into exceptional women. These areas are addressed by God in His Word and call for renewing our minds—filling our minds with God's mind so we think, act, speak, and live His way.

*Your speech*—Jesus had a *lot* to say about our speech. One verse I say to myself every day to help renew my mind—and mouth!—is Matthew 12:34: "Out of the abundance of the heart the mouth speaks." This truth constantly reminds me that what God has accomplished in me on the inside should be evident on the outside, beginning with my words.

> *Speak words that build others up and impart grace.*

Take, for instance, telling the truth. I've put this first on my list because as a new Christian this is where God had me begin my mind-renewal process. As a girl I'd instituted the fine art of "white lying" as a form of "proper" etiquette. Instead of saying no and possibly hurting someone's feelings, I would reply with something vague like "I'll try to be there" even though I knew I wouldn't. As part of renewing my mind, I felt convicted to give up this form—and all others—of lying. I had to constantly think on the Scripture as a reminder to be totally...but gently...honest. I had to put away lying, and let my yes be yes and my no, no. I had to remember to tell the truth and speak it with love and grace and tact.[2] As I thought on God's teachings about the tongue, I set new priorities and standards for my speech—*God's* priorities and standards! The transformation had definitely begun!

Inappropriate speech extends far beyond lying, of course. As we renew our minds with scriptural truths that teach us about acceptable and unacceptable language, our talk is transformed. We find ourselves "putting off" anger, malice, wrath, blasphemy, swearing, gossiping and slander, insulting others, delivering put-downs, and what the Bible calls "filthy" and "corrupt" language and "evil speaking."[3] These worldly speech patterns begin to be replaced as we meditate on God's values and speak words that are good for building others up and imparting grace to the hearers (Ephesians 4:29).

*Your habits*—Some other "old life" areas God pointed to in my life had to do with bad habits such as looking for shortcuts, doing things in a sloppy way...or thinking in a sloppy way ("Eh, it doesn't matter. This is no biggie."), laziness, being late, looking for loopholes to wiggle through to get out of something or to make something all right. Can you relate?

The more you read and study the Bible, the more you discover scriptures that reveal God's standards. Pray and take action! The old ways of doing and handling things have to go. The former ways of responding have to go. Even though bad habits may be deeply ingrained, prayer is your moment-by-moment hope for a makeover. In the place of your old style, cultivate honesty, excellence in all things, punctuality, diligence, and respect for others, including those in authority. "Whatever you do, do it heartily, as to the Lord" (Colossians 3:23)! Doesn't this verse lay it on the line?

*Your attitudes*—The vast territory of attitudes and emotions, such as anger, depression, fear, selfishness, and pride is next. In my reading I found a thought-provoking conclusion in *The Role of Women in the Church* by Dr. Charles Ryrie. This scholar (the creator of *The Ryrie Study Bible*) went through the entire Old and New

Testaments researching the role of women and came up with these two noble, needful, meaningful, spiritual roles: *service* and *prayer.* Prayer, along with serving others, is a better use of your energy than anger. Serving humbly also dispels pride. Helping others takes care of any selfishness too.

God has new ways for us to do things. He tells us to put away our old methods of relating to people. Put away manipulation. Put away moods and moodiness and the use of them to get what we want or communicate what we want. It's easy to fall back into old habits and decide, "Well, I'll just sulk" or "I just won't say anything. I'll just give him the cold shoulder. I'll just mope around until he gets the message." If you catch yourself doing this, pray for an open, loving heart toward others and an obedient heart to God's ways of treating people.

*The exceptional woman—you!—serves and loves and helps willfully, cheerfully, heartily. And she speaks the truth in love.*

What's your Number One wrong attitude in dealing with people today? Name it and then look to God's Word for better ways of handling situations. They're there, right in the Bible. You can also ask for counsel from people you trust and who know God's Word when there's a problem. Set aside any satisfaction you may experience from dealing harshly with someone and causing them to suffer when you're upset. Replace it with prayer for that person and service to him or her.

And negativism, pessimism, cynicism also fit here. A woman in my Bible class asked me what I thought of sarcasm in a marriage relationship. I considered and then I answered, "I think it has to go. Sarcasm only hurts. For instance, today you know your mate is kidding when he speaks with sarcasm, but tomorrow you're not so sure. The same goes for you as a wife. Sarcasm is also a way of saying something you often want to say seriously but are afraid to."

The old ways of relating have to go. The new woman—the exceptional woman—you!—thinks differently, speaks differently, approaches things differently. She serves and loves and helps willfully, cheerfully, heartily. And she speaks the truth in love. As you go through daily life, remember: How you think determines how you act.

## *Remolding Your Mind*

Thankfully God spells out for us two key steps to following Him wholeheartedly. They involve remolding your mind.

*Step 1:* "Do not be conformed to this world" (Romans 12:2). It's easy to admire and want to emulate the "beautiful" people in the world. You know, the famous ones, the ones others look to for their looks, style, intelligence, wealth, or status. But if you look closely, you'll notice that many of the people are lost, confused, unhappy, negative, complaining, selfish, vain, fleshly, foolish, even mean and crude. They regularly live out what the Bible calls evil and foolishness or they're searching for something to make them happy.

Why would we, as Christian women, want to take on their ways and conform to their standards or lack of them? The truth is, *we* have everything—*everything!*—already. Those in the world need Christ. One of our assignments from God is to love, witness, pray for, and persuade them to seek the Lord.

Unfortunately, sometimes we're afraid or too shy to stand out so we blend in, behaving so no one will take notice of us. But this isn't who we are. When we live like who we are—children of God!—we're exceptional. We're different. And not in a bad way, like a showoff or a smart aleck or a weirdo or someone with a holier than thou attitude. No, we're to live as someone quite special, awesome, amazing, and wonderful so others are drawn to Christ in us.

Blending in is dangerous. Why? Because the world is not benign and neutral. The world is Satan's domain (John 14:30; 1 John 5:19). We must be on guard, ready to fight and struggle and harden ourselves so make the choices at every opportunity—at every fork in the road—that enable us to follow God with all our hearts, living an exceptional life in His will and *fulfilling* His will. How?

- *Recognize the command.* Romans 12:2 clearly commands, "Do not be conformed to this world."
- *Understand the importance of not adapting to the world.* You have a twofold purpose that requires you to be different, to be set apart from the world. First, you're to be Christlike, "a little Christ," so to speak. You're also an ambassador and representative for and of Christ to those who live in the world and don't know Him as Savior (2 Corinthians 5:20).
- *Think on God's Word.* This is what renews your mind and leads to transformation. Know God's Word and think about its truths and teachings. Memorize it. Meditate on it.
- *Be on guard.* The world's pull and lure are powerful! And they are off limits to you. You're to "be sober, be vigilant; because your adversary the devil walks about like a roaring lion, seeking whom he may devour. Resist him" (1 Peter 5:8-9). Be acutely aware that the world is truly a hostile place for Christians.
- *Be in prayer.* God's Word, the Holy Spirit, and your prayers equip you for countering the world's pull. Jesus taught us to pray, "Do not

> lead us into temptation, but deliver us from the evil one" (Matthew 6:13). Ask God for His help in staying on the path He's chosen for you.

*Step 2:* "Be transformed" (Romans 12:2). This too is a command from God. When we embrace Christ, we're transformed—remolded—instantly on the inside, becoming spiritually and positionally God's children, blessed with all He does and accomplishes for us. God does all of this—and more—for us. But from that moment until death, we are to nurture what's *inside* so it is revealed on the *outside.* We're to grow spiritually, which will change our ways. Christianity is all about change—radical, revolutionary change at the very core of our beings. We're not to be conformed to the things of the world but be transformed to the ways of God.

## *Moving Forward*

Think for a minute about the metamorphosis of a butterfly. An ugly worm wiggling along spins itself into a chrysalis, the butterfly's version of a cocoon, or retreats underground. And although the changes that occur in its metamorphosis from caterpillar to butterfly appear to be quick, that's not the case. The internal alterations of cells and tissues that lead to such a complete change are gradual.

And so it is for us. We need to commit to nurturing the growth necessary for our complete transformation. My husband tells the men he encourages in their spiritual growth, "God will take you as far as you want to go, as fast as you want to go." So often we can be the bottleneck to greater growth, to change, to transformation, to Christlikeness. God wants, wills, and can take us there, but often we hesitate or impede His work in us.

God wants you to move forward, stay focused, and be committed. He will then take you all the way. Don't dawdle, get sidetracked, or hold back. If you notice yourself dragging your heels or hanging on to old ways that might stall your transformation, take action to get back on track.

This week look inside your heart. If your main desire is to follow God with all your heart, ask Him to show you any areas of worldliness, any areas where you're conforming to the world's standards and not His. Lay your life before Him—every area of it—your dress and speech, your choices for entertainment, your attitudes, the way you spend your money and time, your behavior, and your friends. Then take a giant step toward refusing to be conformed to the world's ways by making the decision to *not* go down that road. Opt to go God's way when you stand at junctions in your life. Choose to do His "good and acceptable and perfect will." And live out your transforming life passionately and wholeheartedly. These choices will lead you to living God's plan for you. And this, dear friend, will make *you* an exceptional woman!

*Self-control reaches its highest discipline in the absolute giving away of the whole life to the care and service of God.*[1]

JOSEPH PARKER

11

# *Renewing Your Mind*

*Do not be conformed to this world,*
*but be transformed by the renewing of your mind,*
*that you may prove what is that good and*
*acceptable and perfect will of God.*

ROMANS 12:2

Can you recall your trip of a lifetime or envision a yet-to-occur dream trip? Mine was a study tour I took with my husband and a group of seminary students to a number of Mediterranean and Middle Eastern countries, including Israel. Planning ahead, I carried along some needlework to fill the long hours of waiting in airports, flying, and riding in buses to our destinations. I knew it would be a good start on a large piece of embroidery and give me the momentum to continue after the trip was over.

When you work on something for *many* months, you never forget that project. The subject matter of that particular needle art was a prayer set in a colorful, cross-stitched border. This prayer hangs on one of the walls at home, encouraging me every day: "Lord, give me the grace to recognize the things which cannot be changed, courage to change those which can, and wisdom to know the difference."

## *Reflecting the Image of Christ*

To become an extraordinary woman of God involves the desire, courage, and energy to change—to grow, to fix, to correct, to make right—those things that can and need to be changed. It involves embracing God's standards and wanting to be transformed from the inside out to meet those standards.

Becoming God's exceptional woman involves finding out what it means to follow God with all your heart...and then implementing what you're learning. This is transformation! As I mentioned earlier, the word "transform" occurs only three times in the New Testament. In Romans 12:2, Paul is exhorting us to not be conformed, shaped, or squeezed into the world's mold. Instead we're to be *transformed,* to be changed into another form. What does this form look like? Second Corinthians 3:18, another verse containing the word "transformed," gives us the answer:

> But we all, with unveiled face, beholding as in a mirror the glory of the Lord, are being transformed into the same image from glory to glory, just as by the Spirit of the Lord.

The process of transformation (or metamorphosis) Paul is talking about in Romans requires undergoing a complete change. But as 2 Corinthians suggests, the process of being changed, with the help of the Holy Spirit, will "transform" us to act more like Jesus in all His moral excellencies. Isn't that a wonderful direction for your life? Wouldn't you like to better reflect the true image of Christ to a watching world? I know I would! And here are some ways to initiate the changes we want or perhaps need to make. And they come directly from God.

### *Changing Your Thinking Patterns*

Change how you think—that's what Romans 12:2 says: "Be transformed by the *renewing of your mind.*" If you're a Christian, you're a new woman. "If anyone is in Christ, [she] is a new creation" (2 Corinthians 5:17). That means your mind is different from the point of believing in Christ on. Now you have "the mind of Christ" (1 Corinthians 2:16). And that should—and does!—make a huge difference.

Think once more about the butterfly. In its metamorphosis, there's an event a caterpillar goes through that makes the major change happen. This is when it goes into a chrysalis or goes underground, depending on the species. During this state of withdrawal and hibernation the profound changes take place in the hidden worm. And *voila!* after weeks—even months, depending on the species—out of sight, a glorious butterfly triumphantly emerges.

And it's the same for you and me. Transformation may start in your heart, but outward changes take place with *the renewing of your mind*. How does this renewing process take place? Here are a few spiritual disciplines that have helped me, and I hope they will help you too.

*Get alone with God*—Like a butterfly, most of our transforming changes will take place in private. In secret. In a chrysalis, so to speak. Underground. Alone with God. Hidden away with Him in quiet solitude, you can exercise this chief "spiritual discipline." When was the last time you spent time with just you and God? No, I'm not talking about your regular quiet time or devotional time. I'm talking about extended alone time for thought, prayer, a lifestyle evaluation, and the making of fresh commitments to Him. The world with all its noise and clamor is a distraction. You need a personal retreat. Why not spend some time this week in solitude with God?

*Get into the Book*—Every time you read the Bible there's the potential for change. There's no doubt about this. An exceptional woman spends significant amounts of time quietly reading, meditating, and memorizing God's Word.

We're continually bombarded by the world. But we can counter its influence by getting into the Book in as many ways as possible. I read that Ruth Graham kept an open Bible on the breakfast table for years. Why? So every time she went through the kitchen, she could read another paragraph or marked passage. She called it "snacking on the Word of God." That's not a bad idea!

As a spiritual discipline this week, commit to meeting with God seven times. Do you believe meeting with God like this can change you? Change your thoughts? Seriously alter your tendency to think worldly thoughts? Replace worldly and human thoughts and fears with God's thoughts? Of course it will! (And don't forget to put your open Bible where you'll pass by it for nibbles during the day. Yum yum!)

*Get the right perspective on prayer*—In my biblical counseling there was a common scenario among the counselees who came for help. As they signed in, they were asked to fill out a questionnaire about the problem that brought them to seek help. One question was, "What have you done about this problem?" Most of the women answered they had prayed about their problems.

Praying is a positive step. However, one of the counselor's targets was to show the man or woman that prayer isn't a magic wand to be waved over his or her problems to make them go away. The focus of prayer in the New Testament is not to be relieved of a problem or situation, but to be strengthened to live with the problem:

- Jesus prayed to be relieved of the burden of the cross, but He was adamant about putting His Father's will first (Luke 22:42).
- Stephen, a martyr for Christ, didn't pray to escape being stoned, but that his persecutors be forgiven (Acts 7:59-60).
- Paul did not pray to be released from prison, but that he might preach with boldness to his guards (Ephesians 6:19-20).

- James did not pray for relief for his readers in their trials, but that they would count their trials all joy and gain patience as they went through their ordeals (James 1:2).
- Peter did not pray for his suffering readers to be relieved, but that they rejoice that they were partakers of Christ's sufferings (1 Peter 2).

Prayer doesn't change our life circumstance or our problems. No, prayer's focus is to change us! Why this emphasis? Because the metamorphosis takes place in *us* as we pray. *We* change. Then, if the situation or circumstance never changes, that's OK because *we* have changed to the point where *we* can handle whatever the problem or situation might be. Remember my needlework prayer? Its message gives the right perspective on prayer: "Lord, give me the grace to recognize the things which cannot be changed, courage to change those which can, and wisdom to know the difference."

*Get the Book in you*—Yet another spiritual practice for renewing your mind is meditating on what you're learning, even memorizing meaningful Bible verses and passages. That's why I keep telling myself, "Elizabeth, make sure you're memorizing Scripture!" Our goal is to fill our minds with *His* mind. Then, when a decision or action is required, we have God's Word—God's voice, so to speak—hidden in our hearts to guide us, speak to us, point us to the correct choice.

You, like all Christians, must exchange the lies of the world with the truths of God's Word. So you need to put the truths of God into your mental process. Then it's always available to renew your mind... anytime...anywhere...in any situation. Memorizing Scripture permanently stamps God's ways upon your heart and mind so you can follow Him with all your heart, soul, and mind (Matthew 22:37).

So why waste time as you drive along listening to the radio?

Instead, memorize and review Scripture and fill your mind with God's mind. Meditate on what you've already filed away and review and think on what you're presently memorizing. Think on the pure, lovely, noble, uplifting, edifying, transforming truth of God's Word. Choose this instead of dwelling on the latest tragedy, crisis, or fad, on some movie, or music star, or a public person's latest conduct, crime, or opinion. Meditate on God's Word *anywhere,* at *anytime,* including in your car, bed, or while waiting at the doctor's office. A glorious transformation occurs when you do!

*Get your growth down on paper*—Another spiritual discipline that I love is journaling. Every word you write in a journal has to first pass through your mind. Even if you're jotting down a quote from someone you admire or from something you've read that you don't want to lose or forget, that person's words make their way through your mind and heart to arrive on the pages of your treasured journal. Writing in a journal or notebook is an excellent exercise for renewing your mind by selecting what is important and valuable enough to merit the effort and discipline it takes to record it, preserve it, and revisit it often. It brings your thoughts captive to the obedience of Christ (2 Corinthians 10:5).

*Show up for worship. This is your appointment with God and an opportunity to hear His Word being taught.*

*Get together with God's people*—And then there's worship, sweet worship! Gathering at church with God's people is so refreshing, so renewing! When I sang in the church choir, I would sit in the choir loft and look out at the church. Sometimes the sanctuary appeared half empty. I wondered, *Where are those people? Where did they go this week? They say this is their home church, but where are they?*

And if there was a guest preacher and quite a few people were missing, I wondered, *Did they call the church to see if Pastor was going to preach? And if they found out he wasn't, did they go somewhere else...or stay home?* God is the God of surprises and blessings. He arranges for us to hear and benefit from many messengers. A wonderful, passionate preacher from Australia...or England...or South Africa...or Fiji might leave you breathless. A teacher of theology might make the profound plain and open your eyes to understanding. A fiery young expositor may challenge you in new ways.

Show up for worship! This is your appointment with God. When you arrive, you'll be renewing your mind by hearing God's Word taught and spending time with the family of God. Getting together with God's people infuses you with the knowledge, courage, and fortitude to go into the next week armed, thinking properly, and ready. You'll be less likely to be conformed to the world and its ways during the upcoming week.

*Get a few close friends*—If you choose to surround yourself and spend time with committed Christian friends, you'll be stronger than if you spend your time with people living in the world (unbelievers). Non-Christians don't *believe* what you believe or who you believe in—Jesus Christ. They have only personal standards for their conduct. They seldom make the choices you will want to as a follower of Christ, and they won't understand the ones you make or why you make them. They won't encourage you in your goals for living for God and following Him with all your heart. In fact, you may even be laughed at and mocked.

If you work at a job in the world for 40-plus hours a week, that's a lot of "worldliness," a massive dose of exposure to the world and its ways. My friend, you will have to be strong and have your mind turned on, to be on guard, to know what you believe, and to have the courage to conform your behavior to God's ways.

Here's an all-too-common scenario. A woman who works at a

job 40 hours a week often spends more time with office workers than she does with those at home. Friendships are formed at work, leading to occasional weeknight activities with coworkers, leading to getting together on weekends, and soon she's doing things with work friends instead of going to church.

Yes, you're to be a friend to all and witness Christ to all. And you're to love and pray for everyone. But, as 1 Corinthians 15:33 says, "Evil [worldly] company corrupts good habits." Your time away from work or community activities is *your* time for participating in godly pursuits, for spending time with your family and God's people, for actively pursuing spiritual growth and transformation.

*Get your heart to talk*—A woman at a conference asked, "Elizabeth, I know the ladies in my church love God, but we never talk about Him. We never talk about what we're reading in our Bibles. We never talk about areas where we're growing or need to grow." She went on, "I love God, but I'm not very verbal. How can we start talking about meaningful things? Important things? Things that matter?"

As we talked I noticed the women around me. They were working on elective craft projects and sitting and gabbing about things women usually talk about. And yet we were at a Christian retreat, a time to separate from the world and center on God and His Word, on Christ and growing more like Him.

I told my new friend, "Start with you. Ask a lot of different questions—not 'How are you?' questions, but ones that draw out something meaningful and significant." I once listened to a tape describing an 83-year-old woman who never said hello to anyone at church but asked first thing, "Have you read any good books lately?" She dove right into something of importance, to what someone was learning and doing in real life

What else can you use to start conversations? Ask others for suggestions for a good book to read, or a Bible study to go through, or a list of favorite verses you can memorize. Ask for help with your prayer life, inquire about what's worked for them, how they find time, or if they have a system or format that helps them.

If you're with Christians, consider it a blessing! Use this precious time to talk about Christ. About your heavenly Father. About what you're learning and how you're growing. Sisterhood in Christ comes with privileges—a relationship centered around and because of Christ and focused on the things of ultimate importance. Your mutual love for Christ will stimulate each of you to love and good works, assisting all of you in the renewing of your minds.

### *Revealing the Real You*

I said there are three uses of the word "transformed" in the New Testament. Here now is the third:

> [Jesus] was transfigured [transformed] before them. His face shone like the sun, and His clothes became as white as the light (Matthew 17:2).

This is a glimpse and description of Jesus being changed from within. Christians refer to this event as "the transfiguration of Christ." He changed. He metamorphosed. Luke 9:29 reveals more: "As [Jesus] prayed, the appearance of His face was altered, and His robe became white and glistening." Jesus was transformed as He prayed. Why? He wanted His inner circle of disciples—Peter, James, and John—to see who He really was—the Son of God.

An exceptional woman needs to be real and not afraid to reveal her real self. She wants to be transformed by focusing her mind on the things of God and His will—the things that matter—things that will cause her to think differently. This renewed thinking will result in behavior that's different, actions that are different, and speech that's different than worldly behaviors and patterns.

## *Moving Forward*

An interesting fact about the metamorphosis of the caterpillar is that while it is in its chrysalis, two things are happening. First there's a destructive process going on that's breaking down some of the organs inside the caterpillar. At the same time a constructive process is going on as some new adult organs are formed. And so the caterpillar emerges after its time out of sight with a body made new. Transformed!

The butterfly's renewal procedure is similar to what you experience when it comes to your growth and movement toward God's will. The destructive process is your decision *not to be conformed* to the world, to break its hold on you, to do battle against it, to withdraw and turn from it and seek something different. The constructive process is *being transformed* to God's standards, your life changing to match the new life of Christ inside you. This is transformation from sinful depths to the exceptional heights found in Christ!

At the fork in the road you'll go *God's* way, do things *His* way, think *His* thoughts, view life and choices through *His* eyes, live for *Him*. You'll choose actions that will renew your mind and make you more like Christ. These choices and decisions make you an extraordinary woman! Are you becoming more like your Savior, the One you love, and the One who loves you? Then you're well on your way!

*If there is a God and He cares for men,*
*then the most important thing in the world*
*is to find out what*
*He wants me to do and to do it.*[1]

Cecil Rhodes

12

# *Following God's Will*

*Do not be conformed to this world,*
*but be transformed by the renewing of your mind,*
*that you may prove what is that good and*
*acceptable and perfect will of God.*

ROMANS 12:2

I've mentioned that for the first 28 years of my life I was not a Christian. But by the grace of God, my life was transformed. God opened my heart to receive His Son, Jesus Christ. And off I went into warp speed, seeking to follow God with all my newly transformed heart. My husband, Jim, rededicated his life to Christ too, graduated from seminary, and went into ministry. The next several decades of my life were spent living as the wife of a pastor, raising my two daughters, and being as faithful as possible to develop a deeper relationship with my Lord.

In those early years I knew little about living the Christian life, so I dug into my Bible for answers. About seven years into my growth, I received a letter from the leaders of our home church asking if I would consider teaching a small group of women as part of a newly formed women's ministry. I'd never taught a Bible class, and I was scared to death by this opportunity to serve the Lord. But I'd studied the women in the Bible for those seven years, so with Jim's encouragement I agreed to teach and, like Joshua, stepped into my challenge.

God was sooooo good! There were only six women in the class, so I wasn't as intimidated. The next session I was asked to teach the same material in a repeat workshop. Since I'd been strong, courageous, and obedient to the first call for teachers, I was less reluctant to agree to a second round of teaching. Still it was a challenge because this time there were 60 women! And the opportunities God brought my way progressed from there. If someone had told me as a new believer that in time God's will for my life would encompass writing and speaking to women across the country and around the world in 17 different languages, I don't know whether I would have laughed or fainted!

## *The Amazing Will of God*

From my story, you can understand why I love Romans 12:2. It's a key to understanding what it means to follow God with all your heart:

- First a negative—"Do not be conformed to this world."
- Then a positive—"Be transformed by the renewing of your mind."
- The result of your efforts—"That you may prove what is that good and acceptable and perfect will of God."

How thrilling! Knowing and living God's will is every Christian's desire and dream. It's what we live for and where we want to live—right in the center of His astounding will! What do we know from this verse about God's will?

*God's will is good.* Romans 12:2 speaks of "proving" God's will. To prove something means to test it, to affirm it. When it comes to God's will, believers don't test it and reject it because it's bad or less than perfect. No, we are assured that if we test it we'll find that it *is* good...and acceptable...and perfect. That's all there is to it! God's will for you reflects one of His amazing attributes—His goodness. You have a good God. His will in your life and for you is always good. That's settled forever. That's the truth. And you can count on it. What's happening may look or feel bad, but it really isn't. It can't be because as a part of God's will it's good. It says so in Romans 12:2!

*This is how you renew your mind. You choose to believe God's truth regardless of your thoughts, viewpoint, feelings, and emotions.*

And you can renew your mind with this truth, this promise, this fact, this certainty, this assurance. You can even say to God, "Lord, from my vantage point this doesn't look so good, and it certainly doesn't feel good at all. But Your Word says it is good, that good will come from it. So I'm choosing to believe Your Word over what I'm thinking and feeling." This is how you renew your mind. It's this simple. *You choose to think God's truth* instead of succumbing to your thoughts, viewpoint, feelings, and emotions. You believe you have a good God who causes all things, including His will, to work together for your good (Romans 8:28).

*God's will is acceptable.* What a lovely word, "acceptable." It means pleasing. Well pleasing. God's will is good and acceptable, and your performance of His will is pleasing to Him. It's mind boggling to think you—and I—can please God!

*God's will is perfect.* People are always looking for perfection. And in God's will we find it. His will needs no improvement because it's already perfect. Like His goodness, God is also infallible and pure—perfect. He can never make a mistake, and in Him there is no evil. *He* is perfect, and *His will* is perfect.

### *Understanding God's Will*

God's will is a vital element in following God. Therefore, we need to gain a better understanding of God's will.

*God's will begins with renewing your mind*—Read the words below several times. Follow them in your mind. Notice that each step you take toward living God's will affects the next one:

> When our minds are transformed,
> our thinking, reasoning, and spiritual understanding are then able to rightly assess everything, and
> consequently we accept for our lives and conduct only what conforms to the good and acceptable and perfect will of God.
> We then prove God's will by choosing and doing only what is good and acceptable and perfect to Him.

> *God's will...*
> *renews your mind,*
> *gives meaning to life,*
> *is unique to you,*
> *requires patience,*
> *calls for obedience.*

*God's will gives meaning to your life*—Life makes little or no sense without an understanding that God has a plan and purpose for your life. When the prophet Jeremiah was about to embark on a difficult life of ministry, God encouraged him by saying, "Before I formed you in the womb I knew you; before you were born I sanctified you; I ordained you" (Jeremiah 1:5). Like it did for Jeremiah,

God's will can serve as an anchor and provide meaning, direction, and significance to your life. Count on God's will whenever you feel challenged or inadequate.

*God's will is unique to you*—If you haven't realized it yet, you're extremely special to God. He created you. He chose you. He loves you. And He's prepared a special purpose for you. You've been given a unique personality, a unique life experience, a unique set of spiritual gifts to be used in a one-of-a-kind way by God (1 Corinthians 12:4-11). Realizing that God has a special purpose for you is a great antidote to feeling discouraged, inadequate, or fearful.

*God's will requires patience*—God's will isn't hidden, but it may take time to become fully evident. After choosing to follow Christ I faithfully accepted the responsibilities, challenges, and opportunities as they were presented, starting with being a godly wife and mom. Don't worry about what you'll be doing ten years from today. Just look around and ask, Where am I today? Your job for today is to be faithful where you are right now. What God has you doing today *is* His will. And more of it will be revealed in due time, indeed with each new sunrise. Enjoy where you are while you patiently wait for the flower of His will to fully open.

*God's will requires obedience*—Discovering and fulfilling God's ongoing will for your life begins with accepting and obediently following His revealed purpose for your life. How will you know God's will for tomorrow if you aren't obedient to His will today? So just for today follow Him with all your heart, as best you can, right where you are, faithfully doing what He's asking you to do this minute, this hour, this day. And then stand back and behold as God unveils the next magnificent step toward His grand purpose for you!

## *Finding God's Will*

How do you find God's will? And what can you do that will help you better know His will, truly believe you're in it, and then live it out with gusto? Some of the steps that follow may seem obvious. And they may sound like repeats. But they are God's sure path to the center of His will.

*Begin with God's Word*—Hopefully you're giving God's Word a reigning position in your day, your time, your thoughts, your dreams, your goals, and your heart. I heartily advise you to never make a decision if you've been out of God's Word for even 24 hours.

It's like this. You go to bed. You sleep a good number of hours (hopefully). You wake up. You're physically out of it—groggy, sleepwalking, staggering toward the coffeepot or teakettle. Physically you have to start all over again every morning. This year I've tried to instill a new discipline when I get out of bed each day (and it even precedes coffee!). I drink 20-ounces of water first thing. I once read that the human brain is 75 percent water and that water gets it and your body going.

The same is true of your spiritual life. Every morning you're spiritually out of it. At each new daybreak you need to begin all over again in your walk with God and following after Him. Let's face it—you've been asleep! So, like the first drink of water, you refresh your mind and heart with God's mind and heart. You need His renewing strength and liveliness. That's what King David said: "O God, You are my God; early will I seek You; my soul thirsts for You; my flesh longs for You in a dry and thirsty land where there is no water" (Psalm 63:1). Your need for God each day is like your body's need for water. You may not know God's will for tomorrow, but as you read and study God's Word, you have His revealed will for today.

*Don't forget to pray!*—I have another guiding principle: Never make any decision without prayer. I've shared in several of my books about the importance of prayer in decision making.[2] Before I make any decision, I create a grid on paper for the issue and prayerfully ask and answer four questions before I make a decision—a decision I hope will lead me or keep me in the center of God's will:

The first two question surface motives—both good and bad.

- Why would I do this?
- Why would I not do this?

These next two questions surface convictions based on the Bible.

- Why should I do this?
- Why should I not do this?

I loved reading the biography of Jim Elliot, a missionary who was killed by those he wanted to minister to in South America. I learned that from junior high school on he felt called by God to serve in the mission field. And finally everything fell into place for him. But to make sure of his calling, he spent 10 days in intense Bible study and prayer, seeking confirmation that it was God's will and not his own.

Bible study and prayer. Before we move on, think about these first two steps and how they affect your choices. Commit to taking your time when making decisions. The bigger the decision, the more time it merits. The more you're in God's Word, the more your mind is in tune with the mind of God, to thinking about things as He thinks about them. And the more you think like God, the more you'll see things as He sees them, viewing your life choices as God does. This enables you to be more certain about coming up with His decisions when making your own. Prayer and Bible study are critical to finding out God's will and moving in the direction of His will.

*Safeguard by asking for advice*—Maybe you're thinking, *But I've read the Bible and I've prayed. Why do I need to seek counsel?* Well, the answer has to do with the heart—your heart. God has this to say: "The heart is deceitful above all things, and desperately wicked; who can know it?" (Jeremiah 17:9). It's shocking to realize that as believers we can read the Bible and pray...and still want what we want. And we can skew and view Scripture to make it say or support what we want to hear or condone. Even after consulting God sometimes we go right ahead and make decisions to please us, not God. By seeking counsel, you get an outside, objective viewpoint. You can ask your husband. Ask your pastor. Ask a church leader. Ask a mentor or mature Christian woman. Ask someone who's wiser and whom you trust. I firmly believe in having a core group of advisors I habitually check in with so I can bounce my decisions and ideas off them.

*Factor in your personal life*—Ask these questions: "Is this a good use of my time or money or energy?" "Is the timing right?" As you well know, there's only so much time, only so much money, and only so much energy. Sometimes there's none available for what you're considering. Or the timing's off. It's the wrong season of life for the kind of commitment you're contemplating. Then go a step further and ask, "Will this glorify God? Is this the way God would want me to spend my time, my money, my energy? Is this a godly cause?" Questions like these help you get to the foundational issues beneath the choices you are about to make.

### *Do God's Will*

This is the granddaddy of all decisions! Choose to do God's will over anything you feel, or fear, or want, or don't want, or have experienced...good or bad. You can study the Bible cover to cover, pray for weeks, ask countless people for advice, search your own heart, and *still* say, "But I had a bad experience the last time I tried this or did that. I said I'd never do it again, so I'm not going to." However, if God indicates you're to do something, then do it! It's better to be in His will and go through a bit of suffering or being stretched than to be out of His good and acceptable and perfect will. Don't miss out on God's grand purpose and plan for you! His use of you will be in unique and rewarding ways. Don't miss His blessings that come to those in His will merely because you want to be comfortable or selfish or safe. Do God's will with all your heart.

## *Waiting for God's Will to Unfold*

God's will is like a spring flower that opens gradually as the days progress. The process begins where you are with what you know or are learning in the Bible. While you're waiting for the unfolding of the future and what you *don't* know, be faithful to what you *do* know. Here are some questions to help you begin to see God's will as you seek to be obedient to what you know Scripture teaches about godly living today.

- *God's will* is that you come to repentance (2 Peter 3:9). Have you?
- *God's will* is that you be conformed to the image of His Son (Romans 8:29). Do changes need to occur?
- *God's will,* if you're married, is that you love and respect your husband (Ephesians 5:22-33). How are you doing?
- *God's will,* if you have children, is that you care for them and train them spiritually (Ephesians 6:4 and Deuteronomy 6:5-7). How do you rate your parenting?
- *God's will* is that you keep yourself pure (1 Thessalonians 4:4). What must be done to ensure this?
- *God's will* is that you be His witness (Acts 1:8). Is this happening? If not, what do you need to do?

## *Moving Forward*

Two phenomenal things happen when you follow God and do His will. First, doing God's will proves over and over again that it is good and perfect and acceptable. Second, it benefits you. Carrying out God's will gives you peace of mind because God is in control and you're where you're supposed to be and doing what you're supposed to do. You don't have to worry about whether or not you're doing the right thing or spending your time and life in the right ways.

Moving forward in God's will allows your confidence to grow, bud, and blossom because God is in control. You're God's exceptional woman so you can go about your duties, take care of your responsibilities, show up at your appointments and events, face the doctor's office or surgery with full assurance that few mistakes are being made in your life. Although you're not perfect—no human is—you're diligently seeking to be in God's will and you're living it. And it's good. It's acceptable. It's *perfect*.

Section 4

# *Becoming a Humble Woman*

*Oh, to be saved from myself, dear Lord,*
*Oh, to be lost in Thee,*
*Oh, that it might be no more I,*
*But Christ, that lives in me.*

A.B. Simpson

13

# *Laying a Foundation of Humility*

*All of you be submissive to one another,*
*and be clothed with humility, for*
*"God resists the proud,*
*but gives grace to the humble."*
*Therefore humble yourselves*
*under the mighty hand of God,*
*that He may exalt you in due time.*

1 Peter 5:5-6

Not a day arrives that isn't brimming with work, activities, duties, challenges, and responsibilities that require a tough faithfulness to get out of bed and move out on God's call to follow Him faithfully with all I have and all He graciously provides. As I tackle my problems, face my Number One challenge for the day, and deal with any ongoing trials and the occasional surprises that crop up along the way, I need God's help and power.

That's why I'm writing this book and sharing verses from the Bible that move and motivate me to follow God wholeheartedly. Biblical truths and promises give me the strength, courage, and power to keep moving forward in running after God and living out His will and plan for me.

### *Discovering a New Kind of Power*

In 1 Peter 5:5-6 there's a surprise. And you may be as surprised as I was when these verses and the message they hold hit me. What drew me to this couplet of verses? For starters, I love the promise at the end of verse 6. That's what first caught my eye. But verse 6 doesn't stand alone. It's preceded by verse 5 and its instructions:

> 5 Likewise you younger people, submit yourselves to your elders. Yes, all of you be submissive to one another, and be clothed with humility, for "God resists the proud, but gives grace to the humble."
>
> 6 Therefore humble yourselves under the mighty hand of God, that He may exalt you in due time.

In these verses we discover a vastly different quality—an opposite in fact—from the strength and power and courage we've been spotlighting so far. In fact, this is a new kind of power. These verses and the virtue they extol—*humility*—can be seen as the velvet side of strength. Read the two scriptures again and note:

- We are called to be submissive.
- We are told to be clothed in humility.
- We are instructed to humble ourselves.

Along with these virtues, Peter also tells us to put on a gentle and quiet spirit (1 Peter 3:4).

*How are we, as God's women, able to capture the power needed to bravely and boldly forge ahead into God's future for us and still nurture and preserve the quality of a "gentle and quiet spirit"?* I wondered. The answer lies in humility. As Saint Augustine noted, "If you plan to build a tall house of virtues, you must first lay deep foundations of humility."

## *Humility—God's Great Virtue*

Humility is actually an attitude. The heart posture of humility is the flower of all the attitudes God desires in us as His women—women who love Him supremely and want to follow Him completely. Nurtured in the heart and mind, humility is an important part of Christlikeness. Jesus said, "Learn from Me, for I am gentle and *lowly* in heart" (Matthew 11:29). The word "lowly" means humble. So we learn Jesus was gentle and humble. Philippians 2:8 says "He *humbled* Himself and became obedient to the point of death, even the death of the cross."

But there's more! A few verses before Philippians 2:8, you and I and all believers are admonished, "In *lowliness* of mind, let each esteem others better than himself" (verse 3). In verse 5 we're told, "Let this mind be in *you* which was also in Christ Jesus." As you can see, *we* too are to be gentle and lowly in heart.

With Christ's humility in mind, let's see what's involved in becoming a woman of humility—in becoming more like Jesus.

## *Looking at God's Plan for You*

In 1 Peter, a book of the Bible written by Peter, one of Jesus' original 12 disciples, we find a *lot* of information based on the great amounts of time he spent in the presence of the Master. (Imagine personally walking and talking with Jesus, and watching Him for three years!) Over and over again the apostle refers to his personal knowledge of Christ.

Peter has much to share! But to whom? He wrote this letter to exiled believers in Christ. They were Christians living in a non-Christian world. (And that's us today!) These scattered Christians were suffering. (Us again!) Peter wrote to exhort them, comfort them, and encourage them. He wanted to guide them in how to live the Christian life under bad circumstances. (What a timely letter for today.)

By the time Peter gets to chapter 5, he's already given much instruction to believers—including you and me—about our relationship to God and to fellow believers. In chapter 5 he turns to our relationships with and in the church. After addressing leaders and young men, he turns his attention to "all of you"...which involves us. Peter tells us a few things about God's plan for us and something we can and should apply to our lives:

> All of you be submissive to one another, and be clothed with humility (verse 5).

### *Three Actions that Nurture Humility*

According to Peter, there are three actions that build a foundation and, in time, characterize humility in a Christian.

1. *Choose to defer to others.* This first action toward humility is embodied in Peter's words "be submissive to one another." This verse is one of the famous "one anothers" in the Bible. It involves action toward others. And please note—humility and submission are *not* part of the fruit of the Spirit identified in Galatians 5:22-23. Humility and submission are not attitudes or characteristics we automatically receive when we trust in Christ. Humbling ourselves and submitting ourselves is something we must do ourselves with the grace of God. So the best first step you can take is to set a goal to nurture humility. In fact, God set this goal for you. First Peter 5:5 is a command meant to be obeyed. To acquire humility and submission we must practice it and we must grow in it.

> *We can submit—bend—because we're certainly not going to break...even though it may feel like it at times.*

And please don't miss this: There's an air of hope in God's instruction to defer to others. Jesus modeled submission and humility for us. Isn't that staggering? That means that you and I, by making a simple choice, by obeying a simple command, will become more like Jesus! And here's another ray of hope. Because it's a command, God gives us the *ability* to respond, to follow through, to develop these qualities in our lives. He doesn't ask us to do anything without providing a way for us to be successful.

What exactly is submission? It's showing deference to others. It involves taking orders. Another definition is "to bend." We can submit—bend—because we're certainly not going to break, even though it may feel like it at times. The goal of submission is to fit in with someone else's plans or someone else's direction. It's to suit or to fit into the lifestyle of someone else. It includes adapting our way to another's way, deliberately subordinating ourselves and giving the other person more authority or grace.

The greatest illustration of someone willing to fit into and bend toward someone else's lifestyle and agenda, was Jesus. This was evident early in His life. Here's the scene in Luke 2:41-52:

> Jesus was 12 years old, just about 13—a teenager. After an annual pilgrimage with His family to the temple to observe the Passover, His parents couldn't find him. He was missing from the caravan that was heading home. When His parents backtracked, they found Jesus still in Jerusalem, at the temple, and conversing with scholars. Mary, His mother, gave Him a little lecture about her concern. Jesus reminded her who He was and what His business on earth was. Basically He said, "Don't forget I am God. I'm here to do My Father's business."

How did this scene end? In verse 51 we find out that "[Jesus] went down with [His parents] and came to Nazareth, and was subject to them." Think about it. Jesus Christ, God in flesh, the Son of God, voluntarily subjected and submitted Himself to the human authority of His parents. He deferred to them, fitting in with their plans and direction. He chose to suit His parents and conform to their lifestyle.

Some time ago a mom came to me about her teenage son. She reported, "Well, he's thirteen. It's happened! He's a bona fide teenager. He now goes into his room, slams the door, and suddenly wants nothing to do with us. He's refusing to do any of his chores or eat with the family." I gave her this reference to Jesus' life in Luke 2 and suggested she share it with her son. I'm sure the results were interesting.

2. *Choose to submit yourself.* Peter said, "Be submissive to one another." We're to submit *ourselves*. When it comes to submission and deference, no one can make you do it. Your pastor can't. Your husband can't. A counselor can't. A parent can't. The church can't. Even best friends can't. Submission is a totally, completely personal choice. *You choose* whether to submit.

Remember that deferring to others is an attitude. This is where the way you think comes into play. So we must always be mentally ready to submit and willingly serve others. Dr. Charles Ryrie writes, "Christianity made humility a major virtue." Then he explains the attitude: "It is an attitude of mind that realizes that one is without any reason for distinction in God's sight."[1] Until Christ's death, humility was scorned, especially by the Greeks, who were prominent during Christ's earthly lifespan. Suddenly, with the spread of Christianity, it became the beautiful blossom of all the virtues for Christians.

3. *Choose to rank yourself under others.* Submission is also a military term meaning "to rank under." A soldier chooses to put himself in subjection to the commands of officers. Like that soldier, you and I *choose* to voluntarily rank ourselves beneath other people.

In the entire book of 1 Peter, 20 or more categories or areas for submission are mentioned for believers. Yet when we Christians think of submission, we tend to focus primarily on a wife and her relationship with her husband. True, Peter does address this in 1 Peter 3:1-6. Like all the virtues God desires in us, humility starts at home with children submitting to parents just as Jesus did and as that young teen boy with the concerned mom needs to learn. But it doesn't stop with children submitting to parents or wives submitting to husbands. We must broaden our horizons when it comes to submission. We must brush aside our tendency to resist or bristle or react against God's command that we live a lifestyle of humble submission. I've heard women say, "Submission? Oh, you mean I gotta submit to my husband. What a curse!"

*All* Christians—yes, Peter says "all of you be submissive to one another"—are to submit in the 20-plus instances, circumstances, and situations he mentions. Submitting to your husband is only *one* person on the list, if that helps put humility into perspective. Submission applies to each believer "submitting to one another in the fear of God" (Ephesians 5:21). And it doesn't stop at the door of your home. This attitude and choice to defer to others extends into the church, to the government, to society, to employers, to school policies, and in the world.

## A Word to the Wise

Shall we tackle the submission controversy? Including the exhortation in 1 Peter 3:1 to wives to "be subject to your own husbands," the New Testament mentions this attitude and choice five more times.[2] As a wife, I've asked again and again, "What does this mean? What does this look like?" And I'm taken right back to the definition of submission: "to rank yourself under other people." Another definition is from *Creative Counterpart* by Linda Dillow. One day Linda asked her husband, Dr. Joseph Dillow, a well-respected former faculty member of Dallas Theological Seminary, something like this: "Honey, from your study of the Bible, just what does submission mean to you?" Out of the vastness of his biblical understanding Dr. Dillow boiled it down to two words: "No resistance." (Ouch!)

We'll see in the next chapter why this is a great definition of what Peter is telling us when he says, "All of you be submissive to one another." But here's how submission works in marriage. I'm to be submissive to Jim. Yes, Jim is in a special category as my husband, and God speaks directly to that relationship. But Jim is one part of the many "one anothers" to be submissive toward. I discovered that once I learned to follow my husband's leadership and laid a solid foundation of humility at home, it was much easier to extend that attitude to everyone else.

## *Moving Forward*

Pause and consider what it means to follow God with all your heart. I'm sure you'll agree that love and devotion are at the core of following God wholeheartedly and hot-heartedly. These descriptive words automatically rule out their opposites—following Him half-heartedly, cold-heartedly, or lukewarm-heartedly. It's easy to limp along in our allegiance to the Lord and in our love for Him. And it's always easier to lag behind and dabble with alternatives, get sidetracked, or put off obedience instead of passionately pursuing God's revealed will. What is His will? As the apostle Paul put it, "Reaching forward to those things which are ahead" and to "press toward the goal for the prize of the upward call of God in Christ Jesus" (Philippians 3:13-14).

*Learn submission from your gentle, humble, wonderful, perfect Lord Jesus.*

We're called and commanded to complete, instantaneous, all-the-way obedience to anything God asks of us. From the lips of Jesus we hear, "If you love Me, keep My commandments" (John 14:15). He also said, "He who has My commandments and keeps them, it is he who loves Me...If anyone loves Me, he will keep My word" (verses 21 and 23).

To follow God with all your heart requires humility. And it just so happens that humility can never be achieved without submission, without humbling yourself. Pride, the opposite of humility, cannot and will not follow God...or anybody else. Pride would never dream of submitting. And "God resists the proud" (James 4:6).

Please don't fight God. You'll lose! Be willing to bend and flex and submit to God's commands...and to the people He places in your path and asks you to defer to. You can do it! All of God's grace is available to you, His dear child. Learn submission from your gentle, humble, wonderful, perfect Lord Jesus. In these days of confusion about compliance and disdain regarding humbleness, go to the Bible for a solid foundation of true humility. Its truths will also bring order out of chaos as far as what God desires for you as a woman who longs to follow Him with all her heart.

*God has two thrones,*
*one in the highest heavens,*
*the other in the lowliest heart.*

D.L. Moody

14

# Putting on a Heart of Humility

*All of you be submissive to one another,*
*and be clothed with humility, for*
*"God resists the proud, but gives grace to the humble."*
*Therefore humble yourselves under the mighty hand*
*of God, that He may exalt you in due time.*

1 Peter 5:5-6

Last year Jim and I were invited to a Spanish-speaking country for a special ministry opportunity. The sponsoring organization was so excited and encouraging that we accepted their invitation and embarked on what turned out to be a thrilling journey. The flight was uneventful (thank goodness!), but what transpired from the moment of our arrival was incredible.

First, we were escorted as "visiting dignitaries" through immigration, which meant not standing in lines, no searches, no questions asked. Then, while we waited for our luggage in a VIP lounge, we were informed that the wife of the president of the country wanted to meet us that afternoon. Next we received that most dreaded of news for a traveler, especially in a foreign country: "Your luggage is lost."

But this wasn't a problem for our hosts. While one group took us to the hotel, another group took our clothing sizes, went to local stores and by the time we were to head for the presidential palace, we were decked out in new garments from head to foot. And that's not even the best part of our story.

When we arrived at the palace, we were met by uniformed guards and a myriad of assistants who ushered us through a labyrinth of back corridors and into a comfortable sitting room where we met the First Lady of the country. We couldn't miss the fact that she was very important. The guards were very much visible from minute one until we left the palace grounds. As this wonderful woman and Jim and I began to talk about our families, she and I even shed a few tears together. I was incredibly impressed by her sweet, humble spirit. She eagerly let me know how God used several of my books in her life and encouraged me to continue writing helpful books for Christians. She also apologized for not being able to attend the conference I was going to speak at. She dearly wanted to participate in the nationwide women's event, but because of her position, felt her presence would cause too much of a stir.

### *Submission, the Beginnings of Humility*

As Jim and I exited the palace entrance with its armed guards and massive gates, I thanked God for the privilege of meeting this lovely lady who was living Christ's life by her actions. Clearly part of her beauty was her clothing of humility. As I'm writing this chapter to communicate how submission and humility work together, I'm pondering my encounter with her. What accentuated this great woman's humility? I saw it in her submission to God first and foremost. But she was also submissive to her husband and his responsibilities, to her country's protocols, to her schedule, to her position, to her responsibilities.

*Submission is basic to Christianity. It is the foundation of relationships, of life in the church, of unity, of peace, of progress.*

Not to mention her willingness to learn from others (even me) as she reads and seeks to grow.

Is her humility a result of her submissive spirit or is it the other way around? Does her submissive heart create the humility I observed? I'm not sure. Humility is a different kind of quality. The moment you think you've found it, you've lost it. And yet you can be the most powerful woman in a nation and still possess its sweetness. True humility flows from a humble heart. And it can be nurtured to the point it becomes so automatic that you never have to consciously think, *I need to be humble or act humbly in this situation or with these people.*

Unfortunately, in many Christian circles submission has been misidentified, misunderstood, and abused. It's sometimes referred to as "the S word." This belittles the lovely posture and mind-set of heartfelt cooperation and compliance that is to mark *all* Christians—male and female alike. Submission is basic to Christianity. It is the beginning—the foundation—of relationships, of life in the church, of unity, of peace, of progress. The subtitle of this book is "Believing and Living God's Plan for You." When the apostle Peter taught about humility in 1 Peter 5:5-6, he was addressing a plan for the church—a plan that works and lives out God's will. Each Christian, each member of the body of Christ, needs to know and believe he or she has a responsibility in the church and then wholeheartedly live it out for the good of all, which sometimes calls for self-sacrifice and putting others before yourself—acts that call for humility.

## A Personal Story

In the previous chapter we ended with a discussion on submission in marriage. We looked at some of the many instructions to all believers to be submissive in relationships. And now, before we move on, I want to share a personal story.

I didn't accept Christ until I was 28 years old. I was married and had two preschool girls. I became a believer at the height of the Women's Liberation Movement in the 1970s. Can you imagine what I thought the first time I heard about submitting to my husband's leadership? *Me? A liberated lady? Submit? No way!*

As far back as I can remember and up to eight years of marriage and three years of being a mom, my life was mostly miserable. Sure there were some good spots, but in general I wasn't happy or content or fulfilled. I didn't have any hope or guidance. At last I discovered and embraced God and His Word—the Bible. I finally had *real* help, *real* answers, and *real* truth! I devoured God's Word and memorized verses that would help me in life, and especially at home.

When I came across 1 Peter 3:1, I memorized it right away:

> Wives, likewise, be submissive to your own husbands, that even if some do not obey the word, they, without a word, may be won by the conduct of their wives.

But that wasn't enough. I needed to know what it *meant* to be submissive to my husband. So I studied the verse. I thought long and hard about what it meant. I prayed about it. I asked other Christians what they thought. Even harder than that was figuring out how to follow through on what I was learning. I prayed even more. The overriding desire of my heart was to do whatever God asked of me, even if I didn't understand it.

So I committed to do all I could to follow Jim, my husband, as my leader. As I did, I learned that most of the applications of submission at home and in my marriage extended to my relationships and roles at church as well. Because of years of practice, continued study, follow through, and a growing understanding of what it takes to make submission happen, I've learned to defer to and serve just about anyone. Here's my partial "S List" drawn from the past and the present:

- I am to submit to God, Christ, the Holy Spirit, and the Word of God.
- I am to submit to Jim, my husband.
- I am to submit to the leaders at my church or any church where I'm involved in a speaking conference.
- I am to submit to those who oversee any ministry I participate in.
- I am to submit to the head, dean, pastor, or chairperson who coordinates any speaking ministry (and that includes their assistants).
- I am to submit to any choir or worship leader… and their assistants as well.

My list extends beyond these, of course. For instance, I have auto insurance because the government requires it. I pay for an annual smog test for my car because, again, the government requires it. I'm on this earth and saved by Christ to serve and follow Him—and be His witness to people around me. I learned how to submit to God and follow Him with all my heart, which led to learning how to submit to my husband, which led to knowing what it takes and what's involved in submitting to others.

Submission is an action, a choice, a lifestyle, an attitude. For me to follow God with all my heart—and for you to follow Him with all yours—requires a spirit of compliance. This is key for *all* Christians—men and women, leaders and followers. It's key for the unity and peaceful functioning of the church. So how do you want to serve people and the church? Do you want to be seen as a difficult problem or as a submissive contributor to the greater good of the many? Do you want to be known as a "whatever you do steer clear of her" person or as a "if you need anything done, she'll do it" person? Humility makes the difference.

## *The Scope of Humility*

On the heels of Peter's call to all Christians—"all of you"—to "be submissive to one another," he gives it scope by adding another divine requirement, which is also a means of complying with his first command to be submissive. We read,

Be clothed with humility.

If you wonder how to be more agreeable and helpful, Peter tells you. While he's already stated what believers are to do—be submissive—he now explains the heart attitudes of humility.

*Humility is an attitude toward others*—It's an attitude of service and helpfulness toward and in the presence of others. "All of you... be clothed with humility" (1 Peter 5:5). Like submission, humility is not granted as part of our position in Christ, and not automatically obtained at salvation. Humility is a quality that we develop as we look to God for help. Clothing ourselves with humility is a deliberate decision.

*Humility is a garment to be worn*—Like me, you get up every day, go to your closet and drawers, and select the clothes you'll wear for the day. We'll need to do the same thing spiritually. Here's a partial list of God's approved wardrobe:

- ✓ Put on the new man (Ephesians 4:24).
- ✓ Put on a gentle and quiet spirit (1 Peter 3:4).
- ✓ Put on tender mercies, kindness, humility, meekness, longsuffering (Colossians 3:12).
- ✓ Put on love (Colossians 3:14).
- ✓ Adorn yourself with good works (1 Timothy 3:10).
- ✓ Be clothed with humility (1 Peter 5:5).

What are you wearing today? Peter says "be clothed with humility." Gird it on. Picture tying on an apron—a servant's apron. We select it, reach for it, pick it up, wrap it around us, and tie ourselves in it. We wear it as a sign of service. When you go shopping and need help in a store, do you look for a woman with a purse? No, that's another shopper. Instead you look for someone wearing a store apron, vest, T-shirt, or uniform and a name badge. That identifies who is on assignment to help you.

Peter wants us to be marked by our "uniform," our clothing, our garments of humility. We are, in the words of author and Bible teacher Jill Briscoe, to join the "Order of the Towel." Like Jesus, who was in the form of God, and equal with God, and before whom every knee shall bow (Philippians 2:6-11), we are to humbly serve others. In perhaps the most tender picture of Jesus in the Bible, we find Him washing the feet of His disciples.

> Now before the Feast of the Passover, when Jesus knew that His hour had come that He should depart from this world to the Father, having loved His own who were in the world, He loved them to the end.
>
> And supper being ended...Jesus, knowing that the Father had given all things into His hands, and that He had come from God and was going to God, rose from supper and laid aside His garments, took a towel and girded Himself. After that, He poured water into a basin and began to wash the disciples' feet, and to wipe them with the towel with which He was girded (John 13:1-5).

Foot washing was assigned to the lowliest of menial servants. Only rarely and out of complete and utter love did equals—let alone superiors!—wash the feet of their peers. So while the disciples argued about which one of them was the greatest (Luke 22:24), Jesus, the greatest among them and God in human flesh, quietly commenced washing the dust, dirt, and filth from their feet.

Jesus' example calls us to gird ourselves with humility and serve others. We need to wrap ourselves in the garment of humility. Put on the badge of humility. Go to work to fulfill God's assignment to humbly serve one another. "Let this mind be in you which was also in Christ Jesus" (Philippians 2:5).

*Humility is a denial of self*—Humility takes place in the mind. Why do I say that? Because humility is lowliness of mind (Philippians 2:3). We're told to "gird up the loins of your mind" (1 Peter 1:13), which is like rolling up our sleeves for action. Our thought process needs to reject the world's ways and conform our minds to spiritually, mentally, and physically carrying out God's commands willingly and joyfully. "Humble yourselves under the mighty hand of God," Peter tells us (1 Peter 5:6).

God doesn't tell us to *feel* humble. He's not even saying we're to *pray* to be humble (although that wouldn't be wrong and is a great thing to do). No, He's asking us to *act* humbly, to give humility expression. We're to do the things that indicate we *are* humble in heart, such as serving others in a lowly manner, taking orders from others, and fitting our lives into their arrangements.

Jesus put action to His attitude of humility. He was willing—and wanting—to serve and help others. He thought of the disciples' needs, decided to take care of the problem, voluntarily wrapped a towel around Himself, stooped, and cleaned feet.

*Humility is active cooperation*—Humility is not passive resignation. And it's not doing something with an attitude because we're told to or made to. We've all seen children do what they were told, whether they agreed or not, but they sure let their attitude be known! This is submission without humility. Our humility is to be actively and joyfully cooperating with others for the good of the whole, using teamwork to get the job done and take care of each other as we follow God's leading.

## *Moving Forward*

Take a minute to think about your life. If you're like most women, it includes:

- a place where you live
- people in your family
- a long to-do list
- friends and neighbors
- some kind of employment
- a home church

Every one of these daily details is a stage set by God for putting on a heart of humility. Each facet of your life and each person in it is a prime opportunity arranged by God for nurturing the beauty of humility in you. So follow after God with all your heart. Submit to Him and others. Clothe yourself with humility. Trust God for what He desires for you. Believe in Him and actively live out His plan for you. You'll never regret it!

*If you let pride enter into your heart,*
*you cannot expect God's blessing;*
*for His promised grace goes*
*only to "the humble."*[1]

# 15

# *Seeing Humility in Action*

*All of you be submissive to one another,*
*and be clothed with humility, for*
*"God resists the proud,*
*but gives grace to the humble."*
*Therefore humble yourselves*
*under the mighty hand of God,*
*that He may exalt you in due time.*

1 Peter 5:5-6

My feelings about travel—especially international travel—are mixed. Jim and I travel a lot. And we love our ministry to God's people all over the world. Each time we go on another ministry trip (usually together), the blessings we receive from the saints override any personal inconveniences and tiredness created by getting there. Both of us are quick to say that some of our most cherished memories have come from interacting with the people we meet on our trips.

As we continue our discussion of humility, my mind returns to a time when Jim and I and our family were living in Singapore doing missionary work. Jim was busy with pastors and church leaders across the island and regularly flying to other countries in the region to do similar work. But I didn't have any area for ministry. I prayed, "Lord, what can I do?" My girls left early each morning for their school on the other side of the island, so I was left alone for numerous hours each day. I'd been very active in the women's ministry at our church in America and had loads of material to teach someone...anyone... but no opportunities came.

Finally I was asked by three elderly ladies to teach them a Bible study in one of their homes. They said they would send someone to pick me up since they no longer drove. To my surprise, a long, black limousine with a uniformed chauffeur arrived and transported me to a penthouse flat in the heart of downtown Singapore. The astounding thing about this adventure was not the limo, the penthouse on the thirtieth floor of one of the most expensive towers in the city, the displays of priceless Chinese art, china, antiques, and furniture, or that these ladies were married to three of the most influential and wealthy men in the country. No, the amazing part was that these women were the most gracious and humble learners I've ever met.

After each of our meetings, as the limo drove me from the riches of what could be compared to Midtown Manhattan in New York City to our little missionary bungalow in a vastly less-than-affluent residential area, I was overwhelmed with the simplicity and purity of the love these three women had for Christ. Their love for God and their desire to be like Jesus expressed itself loud and clear in their lack of pretense, their gracious speech, and their genuine humbleness of heart.

### *Expressions of Humility*

Have you heard the statement, "I can't hear you. Your actions are speaking louder than you words"? Proverbs 4:23 says, "Keep your heart with all diligence, for out of it spring the issues of life." Jesus put it this way, "Out of the abundance of the heart the mouth speaks" (Matthew 12:34). And it's true! We can't hide what's inside. Who we are eventually will be revealed in our speech. And this is even more evident when it comes to the attitude of humility. I don't know about you, but I want to be and be known as a humble person. I want the sweet, lowly quality those dear ladies in that high-rise possessed.

We've discussed humility in previous chapters, but what does it look like in real life? How does it express itself? If the Bible is correct (and we know it is!), you and I can learn a lot about humility by noting the people who possessed it...and, unfortunately, those who didn't. What does humility look like up close and personal?

## Humility Follows in Jesus' Footsteps

In the book of 1 Peter, the apostle begins a discussion on suffering—suffering for doing what is right. To provide a model for his readers to follow, Peter holds up Jesus: "Christ also suffered for us, leaving us an example, that you should follow His steps" (2:21). Suffering is one way we follow in our Lord's footsteps.

I'll bet you don't like this news. No one enjoys or wants to feel pain and hardship. But suffering is a fact of life and one of the surest ways to develop humility. Most suffering can't be controlled. It comes from an outside source, such as disease, accidents, losses, or someone inflicting it on us. What's the humble response when you or I are in the midst of suffering or involved in a difficult, painful situation?

> *Moment by moment we are to respond humbly to pain, unjust treatment, and unkind or untrue words. We're to keep recalling Jesus' example and trust Him for strength to continue.*

Here's a passage of Scripture that shows how Jesus responded in His times of ultimate suffering—when He faced false accusers, persecutors, brutality, and laid down His sinless life for you and me by suffering crucifixion on the cross. This is a hard passage to handle because of the unfairness and the cruelty directed at the spotless, sinless, perfect, and precious Lamb of God, our Savior, Jesus Christ.

> For to this you were called, because Christ also suffered for us, leaving us an example, that you should follow His steps:
>
> > "Who committed no sin, nor was deceit found in His mouth";
>
> who, when He was reviled, did not revile in return; when He suffered, He did not threaten, but committed Himself to Him who judges righteously; who Himself bore our sins in His own body on the tree…by whose stripes you were healed (1 Peter 2:21-24).

Notice the actions, responses, and speech of someone with genuine, godly humility:

- Jesus displayed righteousness—He "committed no sin."
- Jesus spoke truthfully—"nor was deceit found in His mouth."
- Jesus responded appropriately—"who, when He was reviled, did not revile in return."
- Jesus reacted positively—"when He suffered, He did not threaten."
- Jesus proceeded confidently—He "committed Himself to Him who judges righteously."

Like Jesus, our shining example of how to face unfairness and persecution, we are to humbly and confidently keep committing ourselves to the Father who judges justly. Life is not one isolated event. It's a variety of incidents woven together over time. So moment by moment we are to respond humbly to pain, unjust treatment, and unkind or untrue words. And we're to keep recalling Jesus' example and trust Him for strength to continue when we suffer for doing what is right.

Have you realized that three of Jesus' humble responses in the midst of life's pain and trouble had to do with the mouth? Sooooo... it might be a good thing to say *nothing* most of the time. Yes, there is a time to speak up—but it doesn't come around that often. When we hold our tongues on the majority of issues, we'll be well on our way to following God with all our hearts.

### Humility Develops a Servant's Heart

The apostle Paul was one of the most commanding figures in the formation of the early church. He wrote 13 of the New Testament epistles. These letters, written to churches and individuals, provide the framework for our Christian theology, our basic beliefs. In these letters Paul refers to himself several times as "a bondservant."[2]

In the days when Paul wrote, a bondservant was the lowest of slaves. "Bondservant" was the designation for galley slaves, "third level galley slaves" to be exact—those "under the rowers." A slave could not exercise any will of his or her own. He couldn't show resistance to any order. A slave's job was to fulfill the will of another person.

When Paul wrote his self-description, he chose to describe himself as a bondservant. Isn't that interesting? Like Paul, we too are to take on this slave mentality when it comes to following God and serving others. Developing and portraying this attitude is a decision, a choice we make. We have to work at taking on the mind-set of a slave or servant. As slaves of Christ, you and I are to grow to the point of developing a servant's heart so we can respond to God with instant obedience.

### Humility Possesses a Helpful Spirit

Humility is active cooperation, not passive resignation. Humility rolls up its sleeves and says, "Where can I help? What do you want me to do? It doesn't matter how great or small the task, I'm here to help!"

Have you ever agreed to help someone but really had no desire to actively participate? To my shame, I've succumbed to this attitude before and sometimes have to fight it even now. It could be called "resentful resignation." Oh, I was submitting on the outside, but there was no humility of heart, and I gave very little actual help. When people do this, they forget that humility is active cooperation and instead focus on themselves, on what they want or don't want to do, which is the opposite of humility. Yes, pride raises its ugly head. Consider these examples.

*The "last word" woman.* This woman has to have the last word. Her song goes something like: "Okay, I'll do it, but when such and such happens, just remember I told you so." This woman isn't willing to give encouragement or positive input when you need it, but she certainly feels free to tell you after the fact what decision you should have made or how you should have done whatever the job was.

*The "know it all" woman.* Martha, as revealed in John 11:21-39, is an example of this behavior. Lazarus, her brother and a friend of Jesus, had died. Several days later Jesus arrived, and Martha showed her attitude. Whatever happened, her response was, "I know!"

- "Lord, *I know* if You had been here, my brother would not have died."
- "*I know* that even now, whatever you ask of God, God will give You."
- Jesus said to her, "Your brother will rise again." Martha said to Him, "*I know* that he will rise again in the resurrection at the last days."
- Jesus said to her, "I am the resurrection and the

life...Do you believe this?" She said to Him, "Yes, Lord, I believe." *I know.*

- Later, when Jesus asked that the stone to her brother's grave be rolled away, Martha again *knows all!* "Lord, by this time there is a stench, for he has been dead four days."

Yes, Martha knew everything! Even with Christ she couldn't keep quiet. The know-it-all is happy to interrupt everyone to provide correct or better information. You know people like her, right? She's the one who constantly interrupts her husband or friends with correct but unimportant information: "No, Harry, it wasn't seven years ago. It was six years ago." I know...and you don't.

*The "I can top your day" woman.* She says, "You think you had a day! Let me tell you about mine." What she's really saying is, "Don't expect anything from me today. Don't expect me to help plan the next women's conference. Don't expect a very good meal or even a meal at all from me tonight. Don't expect me to clean up. Don't expect...don't expect...don't expect...because my day—not to mention my life!—is far worse or more demanding than yours." Luke 17, what I sometimes refer to as "the wife and homemaker parable," speaks to the issue of the "hard day":

> And which of you, having a servant plowing or tending sheep, will say to him when he has come in from the field, "Come at once and sit down to eat"? But will he not rather say to him, "Prepare something for my supper, and gird yourself and serve me till I have eaten and drunk, and afterward you will eat and drink"? Does he thank that servant because he did the things that were commanded him? I think not. So likewise you, when you have done all those things which you are commanded, say, "We are

> unprofitable servants. We have done what was our duty to do" (verses 7-10).

The point of the parable is that a servant should expect no special reward for doing what is her duty in the first place. Every woman works hard. Wives and moms give above and beyond what they think they can give. And so do women on jobs. This is the way life is. The "you don't understand about my hard day" mentality must be weeded out and replaced with a helpful spirit. A servant's mentality needs to become our very nature, our mind-set, despite all the "hard days" we face. God is happy—and able—to supply His empowering grace to us as we humbly serve others—even after a tough day.

*The "question everything" woman.* This dear woman feels it's her God-given task to question everything she's asked to do (and for some wives this occurs especially if a request comes from her husband). *Are you sure? Do you really want me to do that? Do you really think this is important?* Every response begins with a question. Yes, there are times to ask intelligent questions for understanding and clarification, but this woman questions everything.

*The "reluctant" woman.* This woman is passive. She says she'll help or do whatever you ask, but inwardly she resists. Scripture identifies two kinds of reluctant behavior. The first is open, very visible, and labeled "rebellion." The other is more passive, subtle, less visible, but just as defiant. It's called "stubbornness." Both types of behavior are tagged and condemned by God as sin, iniquity, and idolatry (1 Samuel 15:23). Most Christian women aren't guilty of open rebellion at home, at work, or at church. But stubbornness is all too common. It's seen in:

- *Passive resentment*—We do it but don't agree.
- *Apathy*—We do it but don't care.

- *Indifference*—We can take it or leave it.
- *Substandard performance*—We do it, but half-heartedly and not very well.

The reluctant woman doesn't quite get around to her duties and responsibilities. She says she wants to be a dependable worker, a good wife and mom, a responsible home manager, and useful to others, yet she continually falls short. She makes excuses or blames others for her conduct. She becomes useless to others and to God.

## *Moving Forward*

The descriptions of prideful women aren't pretty, are they? Sadly, though, we often fall into these categories. With this kind of conduct, we accomplish little and don't progress in our service. We're of little use to the Lord and the work—His will—He's called us to do.

But there's hope, sweet hope! Peter says that if we—and all believers—will humble ourselves, God will give us His grace, His favor, His blessing, His power so we can do and be all He planned for us. And this includes you! God wants you to succeed even more than you do. He saved you to serve Him, His people, and others, starting with your family, your church family, and your sphere of influence.

I know you're anxious to know how to get and then keep on moving forward in humility. Here are some ways to begin.

- Memorize 1 Peter 2:21-23. You'll never be the same! This is where the beginnings of humility began for me. You'll be much better equipped to respond humbly when challenges arise when you can instantly recall Jesus' quiet, humble manner of handling suffering and His unwavering trust in God's plan.

- Read through the life of Jesus on a regular basis. I was advised early in my Christian life to read one chapter in Matthew, Mark, Luke, or John every day. This exercise takes five minutes maximum and allows you to read through the Gospels four times a year. You'll be looking at the actions of authentic humility as you draw closer to Jesus' life by reading His story in your Bible day by day. There's no better way to learn about your Savior and His humility! His example will make it easier and more natural for you to follow His humble steps into service.

- Reread the section in this chapter under the subhead "Humility Possesses a Helpful Spirit." As you think about the women who fall short in the actions of humility, evaluate your service, looking for signs of less-than-helpful behavior. Root out the selfishness and pride that cause these behaviors and confess them to God. Ask Him to give you a greater desire for a "gentle and quiet spirit, which is very precious in the sight of God" (1 Peter 3:4).

- Find a woman who is humbly following in the steps of Jesus. Watch her. Study her conduct. Spend as much time as you can in her presence. Consider asking her to mentor you. You'll be fulfilling God's instructions in Titus 2:3-5 to learn from an older, more mature woman of faith, one who believes in and lives out God's plan.

- Remember the truth and promise of 1 Peter 5:5—"God resists the proud, but gives grace to the humble." No matter how traumatic, fearful, painful, or difficult the challenge directly in front of you is, God is on your side. *If* you respond humbly, He will give you His grace to endure as you trust in Him. Those who are humble receive God's grace. (And don't forget the opposite principle: Those who respond, resist, and bristle in pride forfeit the aid of His grace. Even worse, God *opposes* those who are proud and don't listen to or follow Him.)

*He that is down need fear no fall,*
*He that is low, no pride,*
*He that is humble, ever shall*
*Have God to be his guide.*

John Bunyan

16

# Walking the Less-Traveled Road of Humility

*All of you be submissive to one another,*
*and be clothed with humility, for*
*"God resists the proud, but gives grace to the humble."*
*Therefore humble yourselves under the mighty hand of God,*
*that He may exalt you in due time.*

1 Peter 5:5-6

Peter, the man who wrote the scripture above, is famous for continually asking his readers to "remember." Perhaps that's because he never forgot his own proud beginnings with Jesus. Peter was a brash, bold, brawny fisherman. In time he was dubbed by scholars as "the apostle with the foot-shaped mouth." Preachers often attach Peter's name to the saying, "Open mouth, insert foot." It was Peter who confidently asked to come to Jesus as the Lord walked on water...and then after taking a few steps, noticed the waves and sank in fear. It was Peter who declared Jesus as the Christ and then, only a few minutes later, rebuked Him for talking about His death. It was Peter who proudly boasted of his willingness to go to prison or to die for Jesus...only hours before denying knowing Him three times.[1]

At last, by God's grace, Peter learned to walk the road less traveled, the low road of humility, which is humanity's highest privilege. And it's this noble low road that we'll focus on in this chapter. Let's do as Peter advised for a moment and remember what we've been learning about humility and becoming humble women.

So far we've seen how humility works on a horizontal level—the people level. According to 1 Peter 5:5-6, *all believers* are first and foremost to *be submissive to one another.* Contrary to what many think, submission is not a female curse. No, it's a divine, holy calling from God to *all Christians*—male and female, single and married. As a group, all believers are to be submissive to one another and to clothe themselves with humility without qualification and without question. We don't get to pick and choose who we will and won't humbly submit to. Instead, we're to gladly submit to government leaders as in authority, to a boss at work, to the leaders at church, and, if we're married, to our husbands. (And no, this submission is not one-sided.)

To make the task easier, we're to regularly visit our closet and select from our spiritual wardrobe the garment of humility. We're to make sure we are *clothed with humility.* And this is a choice we make willingly and happily because of our desire to follow God with all our hearts and obey His commands.

## *Knowing More About God Promotes Humility*

Many believers shy away from studying theology because they think it isn't all that important or it bogs down in doctrine. But what we know about God determines how we live. If we don't know the character of God, how can we live according to His precepts?

Take, for instance, a person who has an incomplete and inaccurate understanding of the holiness of God. She views her moral actions as being of little concern because, in her understanding of God, He grades on a curve. In her thinking, she's not as bad as the next person, therefore God will understand if she sows a few wild oats, puts herself first a few times, indulges in something not so holy just a time or two. But she is dangerously wrong and will be judged for all her actions (Romans 14:10-13).

Correct theology is vital to *every* facet of pursuing God with full force and living out His plan. Why are we looking at this subject? Because in the verses from 1 Peter 5 (see them again at the beginning of this chapter) there are four facts about God…four qualities of His nature revealed that give us information about Him and direction in our quest for a life of humility.

Fact #1: *God resists the proud.* The word "resists" in Greek is very strong. It actually means that God arranges Himself against the arrogant or the haughty or the proud. It's a military term. God brings His army to do battle against any pride He sees. This is frightening! So take care. God watches how you act, and He will act accordingly.

Jim and I have two daughters, Katherine and Courtney. When they were old enough to do chores and help around the house, one became "the servant for the day" on every even day, and the other was "the servant of the day" on every odd day of the year. That meant that every day one of them was "the servant of the day" to the family. Basically their service boiled down to helping me serve and clear the meals, and if I needed any special help, they were on call. If Jim or I saw any resistance to serving others, we quietly asked them to do additional acts of service. We also went to work on their attitude until a servant spirit became second nature.

This is how I picture this fact about God. He resists the proud, so He too is watching and looking for the prized virtue of humility and submission in us. And when He sees something He doesn't like or notices that something vital is missing, He works in our lives until that area is perfected. Do you want to do battle with God in this area? Then slip into pride and rebellion…and beware! You're destined to lose. The impossibility of doing battle with God and coming out on top should be a very strong motivator to stay away from pride.

Just in case you're not sure you quite understand the nature of pride, let me describe it for you in another way. "Pride" means to raise yourself above others. The word literally means to "show above." It's a proud person who wants to show off, put herself above other people, act better than others.

*Sometimes we wonder what will happen if we humble ourselves in a situation. God promises to help us and give us His "sufficient for everything" grace.*

The ultimate example of pride is Satan, who is referred to as one of the anointed cherubs. Ezekiel 28:17 says about him, "Your heart was lifted up because of your beauty; you corrupted your wisdom for the sake of your splendor." Satan's sin of pride meant he wanted to exalt himself. But God stopped Satan's attempt. God reports, "I cast you to the ground, I laid you before kings, that they might gaze at you." God sets Himself actively against any proud person—even an angelic being!

Fact #2: *God gives grace to the humble.* Now for a positive word of comfort. God tells us to be submissive and humble. That's our role and our decision. And when we follow Him in obedience, He watches over our lives, pouring out His grace—His favor—on us so we can deal with any and every situation we face. That's God's role and His part in helping us live His will.

Just as it's scary to think of facing God's displeasure, it's reassuring to think of God's full measure of grace that comes with our humility. Sometimes we wonder what will happen if we do what we're told or asked, if we humble ourselves in a situation. God promises He will see us through. He will give us His "sufficient for everything" grace. We have only to look to the promise and not at the request that tempts us to bristle or fear or doubt.

Here's a helpful and picturesque thought. In ancient times the word "humble" was used to describe the Nile River in Egypt when it was at a low water level. The ancients would say, "The Nile runs low." By this they meant the water was running within its banks, at a safe, easygoing depth, not spilling over and flooding the surrounding land and causing destruction. Humility is our choice. We can chose to "run low" or we can chose to raise ourselves above others and exhibit pride. In either case we'll reap the results of our decision—pride and resistance from God...or humility and grace from God.

Fact #3: *God requires submission.* Jesus gave us an important principle when He taught, "No one can serve two masters; for either he will hate the one and love the other, or else he will be loyal to the one and despise the other" (Matthew 6:24). Pride and humility are separate masters. Pride is sin and follows the path of Satan, while humility—God's plan and desire for us—follows God's path. Going back to one of our theme verses, Peter says "humble yourselves under the mighty hand of God" (1 Peter 5:6). This is not a suggestion. If you're His child, your heavenly Father asks for your submission and humility. And this is not a bad thing! God never asks anything of us that is evil, that is not for our best. Submission and humility are our loving responses to a loving God, who is gracious and almighty.

Fact #4: *God exalts the humble.* The greatest example of humility is when Jesus—God in flesh—willingly took seven steps in humility, as noted in Philippians 2:7-8:

- He made himself of no reputation.
- He took on the form of a bondservant.
- He came in the likeness of men.
- He was found in appearance as a man.

- He humbled Himself.
- He was obedient...even to the point of death,
- He was obedient...even to death on the cross.

Jesus is the ultimate example of humility, and He is also the greatest example of God's exaltation of the humble, as revealed in Philippians 2:9-10:

> Therefore God also has highly exalted Him and given Him the name which is above every name, that at the name of Jesus every knee should bow, of those in heaven, and of those on earth.

Just as the Father exalted Jesus, so He desires to raise up His obedient children. Jesus first stated this by saying, "He who humbles himself will be exalted" (Luke 14:11). When can we expect this to take place? Peter has the answer: "In due time" (1 Peter 5:6). In other words, when our humility is great enough to withstand the pride of our exaltation.

*All that you've given up or put up with or been deprived of or suffered unrighteously, God will take glorious care of.*

So if you want praise, position, power, or popularity, you might have a very long wait. Forget about those things. Instead, spend your heart and energy humbly serving God, His people, and mankind. When it's time and you're ready, God will do the rest. He'll do the lifting up, the exalting, the honoring, the delivering. In *His* timing—when *He* chooses, when *He* deems best—*He* will take care of everything.

All that you think you've given up or sacrificed or put up with or taken or been deprived of or suffered unrighteously, He will take glorious care of...in due time. He will lift you up, make things right, and make the truth known. He delights in exonerating His humble servants, in justifying His righteous followers.

So wait, dear one! Genuine humility enables you to be patient. Why? Because you're content. You don't need immediate rewards. And what if the rewards never come in this lifetime? So what! No problem. This is not our motivating factor. Regardless of what takes place or doesn't take place here on earth, exaltation beyond measure will be waiting for us in the next life when we reign with Jesus for eternity (Ephesians 6:7-8; Colossians 3:23-24.

## *Taking Steps Toward Humility*

Years ago I taught a college women's Bible study. One of the women came to me after one of our sessions and blurted out, "Oh, Mrs. George, I'm so proud I can't stand myself. How can I be humble?"

I was taken completely aback. First, her earnestness was unusual and refreshing. But next I had to admit that I, along with everyone else, struggle with lapses into pride. Who was I to be telling anyone else how to be humble when I wasn't so sure I knew how either? How would you answer this college student? I did take a stab at it, and as I share my response with you, please understand that these suggestions apply to me too.

*Consult Scripture.* Read and study the humility of the great men and women of the Bible.

- Moses was called by God the most humble man on earth.
- Joseph began as a proud young man, but later became a humble servant who was ultimately favored by God.
- David, in his early days, saw himself as totally unworthy.

- Solomon humbled himself early in life and asked God for wisdom to rule wisely.
- Daniel humbled himself in prayer even as a teenager.
- Mary, the mother of Jesus, humbly referred to herself as one in need of salvation.
- Paul referred to himself as "the chief of sinners."

Go an extra step as you read your Bible. Whenever God opens your eyes and heart through scriptures about humility and snapshots of those who demonstrated a heart of humility, write it down. Begin with a single page of notebook paper—or a section in your journal. Entitle it "Humility," and record the instances you discover. Note what happened, how humility was exhibited, and what the results were. You'll never be the same after this type of study.

*Pray.* When you pray, remember you're not necessarily praying for humility. However, by your very act of praying, you're exhibiting a dependent spirit, which is foundational in the "being humble" process. You can't go through the act of praising and worshiping God in prayer without being aware of your own smallness. You can't go through the confession of sin day after day, prayer after prayer, without realizing your need for forgiveness, which will cause you to be humble. You can't regularly ask God, the Creator and Sustainer of all things, to act in your life or the lives of the ones you love without being humbled. When you do these things, you're acknowledging that God and God alone is the only One who can act on your request and come to your aid. Prayer diminishes pride. And those who don't or won't pray are usually proud. It's that simple.

*Spend time with humble people.* Look around and spot those you consider meek and lowly and humble in heart. Learn from them.

Paul said, "Evil company corrupts good habits" (1 Corinthians 15:33). But the opposite is also true: Good people promote good habits, including humility. And how do you spot those who are humble? Look for spiritual fruit. The branches that bear the most fruit hang the lowest.

*Always take the low road.* When you have a choice, choose a low profile—the less-traveled road. Choose not to be up front. Don't desire to be prominent. Don't always be the one who gets up and shares a prayer request or praise. Take John Wesley's heartfelt prayer to heart: "Oh, beware! Do not seek to be something! Let me be nothing and Christ be all." Jesus shared a wonderful parable about humbleness:

> When you are invited by anyone to a wedding feast, do not sit down in the best place, lest one more honorable than you be invited by him; and he who invited you and him come and say to you, "Give place to this man," and then you begin with shame to take the lowest place. But when you are invited, go and sit down in the lowest place, so that when he who invited you comes he may say to you, "Friend, go up higher." Then you will have glory in the presence of those who sit at the table with you. For whoever exalts himself will be humbled, and he who humbles himself will be exalted (Luke 14:8-11).

Since I learned about the low road and observed it in others, it's been my desire to be in the shadows. Yes, I have a speaking ministry, and yet I've never desired to be "God's mouthpiece." I'm drawn to the women who stayed at the cross when Jesus was crucified. Theirs was a silent service, staying after the fact, quietly taking care of everything, working privately at home in preparation to care for Jesus' body at first light on the third day. If God hadn't named them, we would never have known who they were. Yet God exalted them forever in His Word. These women chose a low profile and provide a model of humility for our own conduct.

*Serve every person you meet.* Seek to serve everyone God brings across your path. See each encounter as an opportunity to show Christ's love. Ask, "How can I serve these people God brought into my life?" If it's appropriate, give them a caring touch. Ask how they are and if there's anything you can do for them. Perhaps you can pray for them. Or maybe they need something you can provide.

*Find the needy.* I had a friend who always went to an event and, as she put it, "looked for the lady who was all alone." She actively looked for the woman who looked miserable. For the lady with no one to sit with. For the lady with a sad countenance. For the lady who seemed lost or perhaps new to the situation.

One day at church I noticed a young woman in a corner crying. I approached her and asked if I could help in any way. She shared her problem, was introduced to her Messiah, and later became a dynamic missionary for Christ to the Jewish community. Finding the needy and offering help is taking a step in humility. Jesus said,

> When you give a dinner or a supper, do not ask your friends, your brothers, your relatives, nor rich neighbors, lest they also invite you back, and you be repaid. But when you give a feast, invite the poor, the maimed, the lame, the blind. And you will be blessed, because they cannot repay you; for you shall be repaid at the resurrection of the just (Luke 14:12-14).

Yes, it's easier—and safer—to stick with the familiar—your friends, your section of the church, your row, your coffee buddies—than to venture out on your own and take the risk of approaching an unknown person. But you'll seldom find the needy in your tight little circle of friends.

*Refuse to talk about yourself.* The next time you walk away from a meeting or spending time with another person ask, "Who was the focus of our conversation?" Here's a hint: If you talked about yourself, you were the focus. Decide that in your next conversation you'll focus on the other person. Ask questions about him or her. Humility always deflects the focus back to the other person. And if you'd like to take this a step further, limit your talking. Listen and take the other's person's conversation in. Nod your head a lot so the person will know you're interested. Remember, there is more instruction in Scripture about saying little or nothing than there is about talking. "Even a fool is counted wise when he holds his peace; when he shuts his lips, he is considered perceptive" (Proverbs 17:28).

*Actively promote other people.* Praise is always appropriate. You can always find something praiseworthy about others if you look for it. Praise people verbally, by name, to their faces, and to others. Give positions of honor and responsibility to others. If there's an opportunity, think, *Is there anyone I can give this opportunity to?* Or when giving credit, *Is there anyone I can give credit to for this good thing that has happened?*

## Moving Forward

So far we've been looking at qualities God desires in His women, especially the qualities that equip us for following and serving Him and His people. We've majored on where to find strength for the challenges God gives us, for fulfilling our roles, and for completing our assignments successfully.

When it comes to being a *humble woman,* you are to move from actions to attitude. Humility is an *attitude* of the mind and heart. You can't crank up humility, and you can't fake it. You have to embrace it, and become it. Allow the biblical reality of humility to become an unconscious response in your life. Paul said, "Let this mind [the mind of humility] be in you which was also in Christ Jesus" (Philippians 2:5).

If you desire to follow God with all your heart—and I know you do—then move forward on the path to humility. Humility is the harder road—maybe the hard*est* road—but it's the right road... God's road.

May God give you His grace as you travel down this less-traveled, most honorable path that follows in His steps.

# Section 5

# *Becoming a Contented Woman*

*The LORD is my light and my salvation;*
*whom shall I fear?*
*The LORD is the strength of my life;*
*of whom shall I be afraid?*

PSALM 27:1

17

# *Looking for Contentment in All the Wrong Places*

*For the* L*ORD God is a sun and shield;*
*The* L*ORD will give grace and glory;*
*no good thing will He withhold*
*from those who walk uprightly.*

PSALM 84:11

"Over the river and through the woods, to Grandmother's house we go" was a Thanksgiving song written in 1844 to celebrate Lydia Maria Child's memories of visiting her grandparents' home. This beloved holiday song originally appeared as a poem in *Flowers for Children* (vol. 2). Today it definitely seems like it was from a different era...but a good one!

My family spent many hours and days singing as we traveled from California to Oklahoma to visit grandparents. But today singing while traveling with family on the way to anywhere has been replaced with DVD players, iPods, and headphones for each child and a CD player for the parents. Times have changed, but the principle is still the same—music or some form of entertainment makes a trip go much more quickly. Today parents don't have to answer the continuous stream of "Are we there yet?" questions as often. Certainly a blessing!

## *Traveling to God's Temple*

The psalmist who wrote Psalm 84:11, "For the Lord God is a sun and shield; the Lord will give grace and glory; no good thing will He withhold from those who walk uprightly," was also on a journey, but not to grandmother's house. He was going to God's house, to the Temple of the Lord. Many years earlier, when God gave Moses His Law on top of Mount Sinai, God required that His people—the Israelites—make annual visits to the house of God. These visits would ensure a renewal of faith and continued connection with the Law. Many "psalms," or songs, were written of the pilgrimages as the people journeyed on foot through the desert to get to the Temple in Jerusalem. In Psalm 84, the journey is almost over. As the psalmist nears the Temple, he conveys excitement, gratitude, peace, and contentment.

Verse 11 has been a great help to me. It's my "contentment verse" or my "everything verse." I've memorized this verse and repeated it countless times over the years, and I'm hoping you too will want to commit it to memory and put it to use during times of worry, restlessness, or discontentment.

## *Looking for a Contented Woman*

One time when I was listening to a teaching CD by a pastor, he jokingly asked his congregation, and especially the men, "Have you ever met a contented woman?" (The response? Knowing laughs and chuckles from both men *and* women.) Sadly, this question is a true commentary on many women, even those who are Christians. Today's materialism sows and nurtures seeds of discontent. The more we have, the more we want. We seem to never be satisfied, so we rent storage units for the old things so we can go out and buy more. In today's "green" culture, contentment with less is a big issue ecologically—but it's even more important from a spiritual perspective. So let's get a better understanding of what's involved in "contentment" and how it factors into following God with all our hearts.

How does Webster's define "contentment"? Paraphrasing, it's "having your desires limited to what you have." We reel our desires in and limit them to accepting what we already possess. A synonym to "contentment" is "satisfied." Another one is "agreeing." And we can extend this last synonym to "agreeing with God"—agreeing with God that everything we have is everything we need. That's contentment!

A content woman isn't worried, upset, or agitated about what she doesn't have or what she thinks she needs or what she wants. Instead she's at rest with her God and her surroundings. Why? Because everything she needs is all that God is and all He has already provided for her!

### *The Opposites of Contentment*

Sometimes we learn more about something when we study the opposites. The following list reveals men and women who were blessed...but wanted more. They looked for contentment in all the wrong places. And their discontent had grave consequences for themselves and for others.

*Aaron and Miriam,* brother and sister of Moses. Moses enjoyed a privileged relationship with God. So much so that God spoke to Moses face-to-face, not through dreams and visions as He did with some others. Aaron and Miriam were not content with their elevated positions as high priest and the leader of the women. No, they wanted Moses' position and favor with God. So what happened? A showdown! God brought the three siblings before Him and condemned Aaron and Miriam for speaking against His servant Moses (Numbers 12:4-15). When God left, Miriam had leprosy. Even after Moses intervened on his sister's behalf through prayer to God, she stayed leprous for seven days. Envy cost these two great leaders great shame (verse 11). Although admirable in her service up to this point, nothing more is said in the Bible about Miriam until her death.

*Achan,* a soldier in Joshua's army. Joshua put a curse on all the possessions in Jericho. Traditionally a conquering army helps itself to the spoils of war. But before the battle of Jericho, Joshua strictly prohibited the people from taking *any* of the booty. Instead, all the goods were to be offered to God (Joshua 6:18-19). Achan, though, was not satisfied with the victory alone. He hid some of the forbidden items in his tent for himself. His greed cost him his life when he was found out...and also the lives of his children and livestock...and 36 other men who died because of Achan's sin (Joshua 7:5,11-12,24-25).

*David,* the king of Israel, was an extremely successful king. He conquered many lands and people, built splendid homes, and had numerous wives. Yet even with all this, he was not content. One evening he happened to see a beautiful woman named Bathsheba bathing on a rooftop below his palace. He inquired about her, had her brought to him, and then he committed adultery with her. Not only did David violate Bathsheba, but he sinned grievously against God. The consequences? His kingdom, starting with his own family, was in turmoil for the remainder of his reign (2 Samuel 11–12).

*Persian leaders.* Daniel, an Israelite, and some Persians were leaders in the government of Darius, the king of Medo-Persia. Because of God's favor, Daniel distinguished himself. Rather than accept Daniel's exaltation, the disgruntled officials sought a way to bring him down. You probably know the story. Daniel was charged with praying to God rather than to the king. The young Hebrew was thrown into the lions' den...where God miraculously shut the mouths of the beasts and saved Daniel's life. When the plot was exposed, all the Persian leaders where thrown into the lions' den and eaten! Their frustration and discontent cost them their lives (Daniel 6).

## *Settling the Issue of Discontentment*

I certainly don't want to go through destroyed family relationships, leprosy, turmoil, or death by lions because of a lack of contentment. And I'm sure you don't want to either! So how can you and I be or become women who limit our desires to what we have? Who are satisfied with life as it is, realizing everything has come from the hand of God? Who agree with Him that we have all we need. How can we stop worrying, stop being agitated about the things in life—things we have, don't have, or want? How can we be simply and deeply content believing there are no unmet needs in God's economy?

I struggled with these questions for several years after Jim quit his wonderful, high-paying corporate job to attend seminary in preparation for a life of ministry. You see, we'd finally made it. We had a nice house, nice cars, and a nice income. Jim was routinely being promoted, and life was looking rosy...from a materialistic viewpoint. But, praise God, we met Jesus! How exciting the times were as we began to change in our hearts and in our family. Love, joy, and peace reigned all around. But something else changed too. When Jim quit his job to follow God's leading, we sold the nice house and one of the cars to cover his tuition, and we moved into a really small house, about the size of the garage we had before.

I didn't...and don't...regret the decisions we made during that time. But that didn't keep me from occasionally looking back at what we'd left and becoming a little restless (and on some days a little resentful) with what I'd given up...and a little fearful about the future.

I remember sitting in a seminary wives group and hearing a wise, seasoned pastor's wife say, "As a pastor's wife, you will probably never have as much money as the people in your congregation, so just settle that right now." How I needed to hear that...and accept it.

Another thing I did that I shouldn't have done was look longingly at my neighbor's life. Her husband left for work every morning at 7:55 and came home at exactly 5:05 five days a week. My Jim left for seminary at 5:00 and then went to the church and worked after his day of classes. Then he participated in pastoral visitations until 9 or 10...and held two other jobs on the weekends. There were some long, dark days and nights for me.

## *Turning the Corner to Contentment*

But God was, as always, faithful. He came to my rescue and answered my questioning heart with Psalm 84:11: "For the Lord God is a sun and shield; the Lord will give grace and glory; no good thing will He withhold from those who walk uprightly." This verse is precious and priceless! It reveals provisions from God that gave me great peace and contentment so many years ago and continues to minister to me each and every day. This verse helped me turn an important corner in my thinking and in my heart. It contains five reasons why you and I can be content. Here are two of them, with more to come...so stay tuned!

*Reason #1—God is a sun.* Any course on how to study the Bible will tell you that the number of times a word or phrase is used is significant. When either is used only once or twice, it has *major* significance. "The Lord God is a sun" is used only one time in the entire Bible—and it's right here in Psalm 84. If I asked you what the sun means to you or to list all the things the sun is and does, your answers might range from the scientific to the spiritual. The sun means everything to our planet. All provision for food and life and energy is a direct result of the sun, which is a result of God's creative power.

Since moving to the Seattle area (after living 35 years in sunny Southern California), I've developed a much more serious appreciation for the sun. The ever-present mist in the Pacific Northwest is perfect for a husband/wife writing team. But if we're not careful, we can have a down day (or two!) after not seeing the sun for many days...and sometimes months.

But I thank God that even when we don't have the physical sun, we have the Lord God as a sun! Here are a few of the benefits of the physical sun and how God, as your sun, provides for you spiritually:

> *God is perfectly, 100-percent capable of meeting your needs, whether they are physical, spiritual, emotional, mental, financial, or social.*

- The sun brings joy, warmth, and energy. Psalm 30:5 says, "Weeping may endure for a night, but joy comes in the morning." Like the sun, the Lord's presence in your life brings great joy.
- The sun brings routine. You can set your watch by the morning sunrise. You can also depend on God, who is the same yesterday, today, and tomorrow (Hebrews 13:8).
- The sun brings light to guide you. David said, "You are my lamp, O LORD; the LORD shall enlighten my darkness" (2 Samuel 22:29). Even in the dark, you have the glory of the Lord to light your path.
- The sun brings relief from the darkness. Darkness causes fear. It brings great anguish for many who are fearful of the dark, the unseen, and the unknown. The psalmist says, "If I say, 'Surely the darkness shall fall on me,' even the night shall be light about me; indeed, the darkness shall not hide from You, but the night shines as the day; the darkness and the light are both alike to You...And in Your book they all were written,

the days fashioned for me, when as yet there were none of them" (Psalm 139:11-12,16).

- The sun brings healing. Before the age of wonder drugs, my mother took my oldest brother to the sunny state of Arizona for six months because he was dangerously ill from pneumonia. Malachi 4:2 says, "The Sun of righteousness shall arise with healing in His wings." Not only is physical healing promoted by the sun, but there is spiritual healing in the Messiah's righteousness.

- The sun brings emotional well being. States that have a lot of cloudy, gray, wet weather have high rates of suicide. That's why so many who live in these states need to take sun breaks in warmer, drier climates. With or without the sun, and with or without sun breaks, Psalm 30:11 tells you that God can turn your gloom into gladness: "You have turned for me my mourning into dancing; You have put off my sackcloth and clothed me with gladness."

If the physical sun is this significant, and God made the sun, then He is perfectly, 100-percent capable of meeting your needs, whether they are physical, spiritual, emotional, mental, financial, or social.

Now you know why the psalmist who wrote Psalm 84 was so content as he trekked toward Jerusalem! He was thinking about God. He was praising God. He was worshiping God. So the next time you're feeling a little restless about your limitations or what you don't have or what you think you should have, look up at the sun. Then look to the God who made the sun and remember His unlimited provision for your every need.

*Reason #2—God is a shield.* The psalmist who penned Psalm 84 is a civilian. He's not a soldier, but he knew well what a shield could do in terms of lifesaving protection and safety. As he travels on his pilgrimage to the Temple of the Lord, he's thinking about God's loving defense against all the perils that could possibly come to him on such a long journey: "The LORD God is a sun *and shield."* If the Lord as our sun gives us encouragement, then God as our shield gives us confidence for the battles of life:

- The shield was the chief defensive weapon of a warrior. It was his greatest protective asset in battle.
- The shield gave the warrior confidence as he entered battle.
- The shield gave him power to oppose his enemy.
- The shield gave him assurance of being able to conquer his foes.
- The shield gave him deliverance from his enemy.
- The shield gave him victory over fears.
- The shield gave him protection from flaming missiles.
- The shield gave him cover from the scorching sun.

How wonderful to know that God is your shield! You can't see Him, but that doesn't mean He isn't defending you. That's what Psalm 84:11 is saying! When do you need a shield? Answer: In times of danger. And you can count on God for protection. Just as the sun takes care of fear when you can't see what's ahead in the dark, the shield takes care of reality, of what is really here.

There are a few more verses that speak of God as a shield. All but the last one was penned by David, a mighty warrior who had intimate knowledge of shields and warfare. He had his own shields, I'm sure, but he also knew God was his ultimate protection.

- "He is a shield to all who trust in Him...You have also given me the shield of Your salvation" (2 Samuel 22:31,36).
- "For you, O LORD, will bless the righteous; with favor You will surround him as with a shield" (Psalm 5:12).
- "He is a shield to those who walk uprightly" (Proverbs 2:7).

Lets summarize the first two aspects of God's provision embedded in Psalm 84:11: God is a sun and a shield. Our psalmist pilgrim needed both elements of God's help...and so do you. As the sun provided warmth from the cold to those on their holy journey, God provides the warmth of His presence to encourage you when things start getting difficult. And as shields were needed for protection so that no foes could waylay God's faithful on their way to worship in Jerusalem, so God is your protection against the foes that come your way in life. The psalmist had everything he needed for a successful journey...and so do you.

During a time of reflection and thanksgiving, why not thank God for being your bright sun and ever-present shield? Here's a powerful prayer:

> Lighten our darkness, we beseech thee, O Lord; and by thy great mercy defend us from all perils and dangers of this night.[1]

## *Moving Forward*

Isn't it wonderful to be a child of God and be assured that God is your sun? And to have confidence that God is your shield, your protector? Pause now and talk to God.

❧ *Take time* to thank God for already providing all you need for your present well being.

❧ *Take a moment* to reflect on the importance of the physical sun to your existence. Then reflect on the importance of God to your life. One affects you physically and only during this lifetime. Your relationship with God, however, is for eternity! If you think your need for the physical sun is important, evaluate your need for the eternal God who made the sun. He sent His Son—the Son of righteousness—so you can have an eternal relationship with Him (John 3:16).

❧ *Take action* on what you now know of God's provision as both sun and shield. Be content with the limitless provision of the sun and the steadfast protection of the shield. Don't wear yourself out struggling about the "stuff" of this life when you possess something far greater that will not fade or disappear. You can stop looking for contentment in all the wrong places because you now know the right place—God!

*It is God to whom and with whom we travel,*
*and while He is the end of our journey,*
*He is also at every stopping place.*

Elisabeth Elliot

18

# *Living with Grace and Glory*

*For the* LORD *God is a sun and shield;*
*The* LORD *will give grace and glory;*
*No good thing will He withhold*
*from those who walk uprightly.*

PSALM 84:11

One afternoon when we lived in California, my husband and I were driving home and Jim's pager went off. He looked at it, smiled like only a dad can smile when his daughter calls, and exclaimed, "It's Katherine!" Because we were just a few blocks from home, Jim didn't answer the phone. Three minutes later we pulled up to our house, and police cars were everywhere! All the lights were on in the house, and the neighbors were out in full force.

As the story unfolded, we learned that Katherine had come home from work, gone into the bathroom, and as she was coming out, a man was standing in the hall! He immediately put her on the defensive by asking, "Are you the burglar? Someone's robbing this house. Are you robbing this house?"

"No, I'm not robbing this house. I live here!" Katherine replied.

Then the clever guy said, "Well, I'm going to chase the burglars that are robbing your house! Quick, give me your phone number, and when I catch them I'll call you and bring everything back!" Well, she gave him our phone number, and he took off.

Katherine then noticed the back door was missing. Evidently three men had removed the door so they could make the robbery go faster. They were taking things out that open doorway and were coming back for another load when Kath came in the front door. That's when the first two ran away, leaving this third man. All three men got away.

I don't have to tell you that after this episode with the burglars, we spent much time on our knees thanking God for His protection of Katherine during that ordeal. We kept saying to our daughter, "Do you realize what could have happened? Do you realize how God protected you? Isn't it great that you are never out of His sight!" To this day we praise God for His divine shield of protection on our daughter that frightening day.

*Contentment means living in a hostile world with the peaceful assurance that God is truly our sun and our shield.*

What this experience reemphasized to our family is that contentment is more than having possessions. Contentment is more than what we have and don't have. It encompasses what we experience and don't experience. As a family, we learned what it means to be content even knowing the dangers of living in Los Angeles. The burglary was a traumatic event that could have been a lot worse—even a tragedy. But even then the lesson would be the same: Contentment means living in a hostile world with the peaceful assurance that God is truly our sun and our shield.

As we ended the last chapter, we were keying in on two life-changing facts about God that translate into two reasons we can be content in our circumstances:

*Reason #1*—the Lord God is our sun

*Reason #2*—the Lord God is our shield

Now let's move to the third reason for being content.

*Reason #3—God gives us grace.* You and I can enjoy a heart of contentment regardless of what's happening to us or going on around us because we know we have God's grace. Psalm 84:11 says,

> For the LORD God is a sun and shield;
> the LORD will give grace...

Grace! I'm sure you've heard, sung, and read many definitions for grace, including unmerited favor, everything that is spiritually good, something God gives to us that we don't deserve. But here's my favorite description: "Divine bestowment exactly according to human necessities." In other words, whatever we need, grace is given by God for that need.

When do we need grace? The answer begs another question: What are you facing today? That's how much grace God gives—enough to face, handle, and endure what's in front of you. Consider some events that you or someone you know has faced or will face:

- a doctor's appointment to see if a biopsy or surgery is needed
- a trip to the hospital for a test as a follow-up to cancer treatment
- teaching a woman's Bible study for the first time...and tonight is the night
- the school principal calling to inform you your son or daughter is in trouble
- your son calling to say he's getting a divorce and the kids will live with his soon-to-be ex-wife

This list of unpleasant and potentially serious occurrences could go on and on: lost jobs, lost income, lost health, lost parents, lost kids. Every wife, mother, grandmother, aunt, and sister faces these sorts of issues, some even daily. The beauty of God's grace is that it's given *exactly* according to your need. It's *exactly* what you need right now, it's *exactly* here when you need it, and it's *exactly* the right amount.

One woman shared with me recently about her myriad medical tests and biopsies and surgeries that all came at a time when her husband was out of work. She wrote that she knew when she got on the operating table that God's grace would be there at that moment. And that whatever the outcome of the many surgeries, she could, by God's grace, function as a wife and mom and homemaker through it all without worry. She was totally content with the assurance and reality of God's grace. What an example for us!

### *What Does Grace Do?*

We know God's grace is given and granted. We've also noted it is exactly what we need when we need it. But what does grace do besides equip us to get through hard times? What does God's grace accomplish? Hang on...and get ready to count your blessings!

*God's grace saves you.* The Bible says we "all have sinned and fall short of the glory of God" and "the wages of sin is death" (Romans 3:23 and 6:23). We deserve death. In fact we've earned it. Truly this is bad news. But praise God! By His grace He offers us salvation: "For by grace you have been saved through faith" (Ephesians 2:8). God's grace is poured out on you through Jesus Christ. As one hymn writer expressed it, "Marvelous, infinite, matchless grace, freely bestowed on all who believe."[1]

*God's grace guides you.* Paul said, "By the grace of God I am what I am, and His grace toward me was not in vain" (1 Corinthians 15:10). No matter what your background or past or the challenges that stand in your path, God patiently guides you by His grace. Sometimes you can't or won't see the road signs, but His grace ultimately moves you to where you need to be, sometimes gently... and sometimes not so gently. God has a plan for you, and He means for you to live it out.

*God's grace empowers you.* Life is not always pleasant, but God's grace covers you. That's what Jesus said to the apostle Paul when he begged to have his "thorn in the flesh" taken away: "My grace is sufficient for you, for My strength is made perfect in weakness" (2 Corinthians 12:9). God's grace was enough to see Paul through that trial and all that would come in his lifetime. And, like Paul, whatever you now face or ever will face, you can count on God! He'll give you His grace via His power to make it through. You can be content and at peace because God's grace provides all you need now and forever. The psalmist believed and professed, "The LORD will perfect that which concerns me" (Psalm 138:8). "I will cry out to God Most High, to God who performs all things for me" (Psalm 57:2).

*God's grace is sufficient for you.* "Sufficient" is a tremendously comforting word that means ample, enough, adequate. You have all you need and require through God's grace. You have grace that is:

- sufficient for your salvation
- sufficient to shape and mold you into the person you need to be to serve God, your family, your church, and your world
- sufficient to see you through any issue you will have to deal with or any need you will experience
- sufficient to see you home to glory

*Reason #4—God gives us glory.* Psalm 84:11 says,

> For the LORD God is a sun and shield;
> the LORD will give grace and glory.

You can be content not only because of the sufficiency and power of God's grace, but also because the Lord gives you glory. Close your eyes and say the word out loud: "glory." Just saying it gives you such hope! That's because glory has to do with the future or the end of life as we know it. At the end of the journey, when God welcomes us home to life in His immediate presence, oh, that will be glory! It is the reward of eternity. Glory, or heaven, is grace nurtured and brought to infinite perfection. We have all of God's grace for today, all of it along the way, which equals glory in the future. And that glory comes when we see Jesus face-to-face. That's when we'll have His name written on our foreheads (Revelation 22:4). And that's when we'll finally be with Him, worship in front of Him, and reign with Him forever.

### *Understanding God's Glory*

We'll experience God's glory in the future, but we can have some understanding of it today, which contributes mightily to our sense of contentment in the present.

*God's glory is His awesome presence.* Moses asked God, "Please, show me Your glory." And God allowed His glory to pass by as Moses was safely hidden between two rocks, for, as God explained, "You cannot see My face; for no man shall see Me, and live" (Exodus 33:18-20). God is majestic and complete in miraculous wonder, omnipotence, and perfect beauty. When God met with Moses on the mountain, there were thunderstorms, smoke, and earthquakes. God Almighty is a consuming fire, and the reaction of the people that day was utter terror. God's glory is all-consuming.

*God's glory is a display of His nature.* Glory is the manifestation of God's character—His ultimate power and moral perfection. When God passed before Moses, He made this statement about His glory: "I will make all My goodness pass before you, and I will proclaim the name of the LORD before you. I will be gracious to whom I will be gracious, and I will have compassion on whom I will have compassion" (verse 19).

God is completely above all He created. Yet He revealed Himself to Moses and was represented to the Israelite nation in pillars of cloud and fire (Exodus 13:21). He was also present in the Tabernacle and Solomon's Temple so He could be worshiped. And there's one more place where God's glory is displayed.

*God's glory is displayed in Christ.* The only time Jesus revealed His glorious heavenly nature while He was on earth was on the Mount of Transfiguration. As Peter, James, and John looked on, "He was transfigured before them. His face shone like the sun, and His clothes became as white as the light" (Matthew 17:2). If God's glory is the sense of His awesome presence, the more we understand of Jesus and His mission and work on earth, the more we will be aware of God's glory. For in Christ, God's glory was physically present on the earth.

## *Reflecting God's Glory*

Aren't you excited to know you're going to experience God's glory in the future? How incredible! But do you realize you can reflect His glory now too? Think about this: What did Jesus mean when He prayed these words to the Father on behalf of His disciples the night before the crucifixion?

> I pray for them. I do not pray for the world but for those whom You have given Me, for they are Yours. And all Mine are Yours, and Yours are Mine, and I am glorified in them (John 17:9-10).

Jesus was saying that His immediate disciples—and you and me and all His present-day followers—can represent His glory to the world. He is glorified in us! This is a thought-provoking truth.

Jesus is present in the world through *us*. Are you wondering as I am, *Does my life accurately reveal Jesus' character to others? And how can I more accurately reveal the character and nature of Jesus?* The answer lies in a verse we looked at earlier—

> But we all, with unveiled face, beholding as in a mirror the glory of the Lord, are being *transformed* into the same image from glory to glory, just as by the Spirit of the Lord (2 Corinthians 3:18).

The answer lies in transformation! As you understand and obey the truths in Scripture, you are gradually being changed with the help of the Holy Spirit from one level of spiritual maturity to another so you can follow Christ more closely. Becoming more Christlike (reflecting His glory) is a progressive experience. The more you emulate Christ, the more you will become like Him...and the more accurately you will reflect His glory.

## *Moving Forward*

*God's grace and glory*. These are two provisions God gives you as His child. His grace is limitless. It has no beginning and no end. It covers and spans your entire life. As you transition through each phase, His grace is ever-present and always sufficient. You will never face anything His grace can't or won't cover. And when your life on this earth is done, His glory is waiting for you on the other end, on the shores of heaven...forever.

God's grace and glory are wonderful blessings to anticipate, but what about today? Please don't forget the opportunity you have to live out today's challenges in a God-honoring way. Count on His grace and reflect His glory in your actions and attitudes every day. God's grace and glory—these blessings—are yours today. They are here for your contentment today. They will help you follow God with all your heart today—no matter what.

So here's the Number One way to move forward: Read daily in

the Gospels about the life of Jesus. Through Christ's life you'll gain a better understanding of how wonderful God is and what He is really like. As your knowledge of Him deepens, your life will be changed for the better. As Paul said, you will experience spiritual growth as you behold and live in the glory of the Lord. You will be transformed into the same image from glory to glory by the Spirit of the Lord.

*God oftentimes withholds riches and honours, and health of body from men... Honours and riches and bodily strength, are none of God's good things; they are of the number of things indifferent which God bestows promiscuously upon the just and unjust, as the rain to fall and the sun to shine. The good things of God are chiefly peace of conscience and the joy in the Holy Ghost in this life.*

Charles H. Spurgeon

19

# *Traveling the Road to Contentment*

*For the* LORD *God is a sun and shield;*
*the* LORD *will give grace and glory;*
*no good thing will He withhold*
*from those who walk uprightly.*

PSALM 84:11

"If you don't know where you're going, any road will get you there" is a haunting statement that's been in my mind for many years. Another way to say this is, "If you wake up each morning with no clue as to how you're going to spend your day, you'll become a victim of the urgent rather than a master of the important." What do these statements have to do with contentment? And don't goals, desires, and ambition contradict the idea of being content?

I'm a big fan of having goals. My positive attitude in this regard began several decades ago. I can still remember the first serious goal-setting session Jim and I had. It took us an entire Sunday afternoon to create 1-year, 5-year, 10-year, and lifetime goals. As I was writing my ten-year goals, I let out a huge "Eek!" that made Jim almost fall out of his chair. I'd come to the realization that in the next ten years I could expect certain natural and normal things to happen. During those ten years both of my daughters could get married. That would mean Jim and I would be "empty nesters" and maybe even grandparents! My parents, who were then in their eighties, could die. My thoughts went through several other possible scenarios related to life, marriage, health, and ministry.

As I was writing goals and thinking about them in terms of time, it hit me hard just how many life-altering events could happen in a person's near and distant future. I was a little shaken...until I remembered Psalm 84:11 and what we've been talking about in this section of the book:

> For the LORD God is a sun and shield;
> the LORD will give grace and glory.

My heart settled down as I acknowledged once again that God would be a sun and a shield for me. His grace would prepare me and accompany me through whatever was to come. Once I calmed down, I regained that quiet assurance and contentment that comes from believing and trusting in the promises of God. God is in control—everything will be all right. What a blessing the promises of this verse are!

Well, sure enough, in the next 10 years my parents both died... and God's grace was there. And sure enough, both of my daughters were married (one year to the day apart—another "Eek!")... and God's grace was there. And sure enough, a multitude of other challenges came along, such as major surgeries, cancer scares, a grandchild with a physical problem, an offer to write a book, learning how to write a book—things I didn't dream of at the time but that turned my life in new and dramatic and sometimes difficult directions...and God's grace was there.

### *Goals Versus Contentment*

Before we move on to the fifth reason why we can be content, as seen in Psalm 84:11, I want to share my perspective on how goals and contentment are not contradictions. Instead they can be companions that assist us on our road to following God with all our hearts. But there is one qualifier. Your goals must not violate Scripture. I'm sure you've seen or read about people who have scratched and clawed their way to the top of corporate ladders or industries. Anyone and everyone who got in their way were muscled aside as they climbed over them and stomped on them on their way to the top. This isn't the kind of ambition and goals we're dreaming of. No, the goals we're interested in involve *godly* ambition.

Godly ambition is your desire to serve God and spend your life and energy fulfilling all His will. One of my favorite life verses describes what it means to follow God with all your heart. God says, "I have found David the son of Jesse, a man after My own heart, *who will do all My will*" (Acts 13:22). As I share some of the benefits of having goals, keep God's definition of a man—or woman!—after God's own heart in mind, and remember to take care and pray over your goals so they are in keeping with your God-given roles and responsibilities, which we'll look at in the next chapter.

*Goals provide direction.* Goals move your thoughts from day-dreams to concrete data. Goals are statements about the future—what you believe may be the direction God's will is taking you. Goals bring the future (if the Lord wills…or if it is the Lord's will) into the present so you can do something about God's future for you today. Not having any idea or very little idea of your life direction can cause you to worry and become restless. Goals allow you to make confident plans about your future and the future of your family, which will bring contentment. Do you know what Proverbs 3:5 and 6 says? As you read these verses now, notice that the writer's desire is for God's direction as he travels through life.

> Trust in the LORD with all your heart, and lean not on your own understanding; in all your ways acknowledge Him, and He shall direct your paths.

*Goals provide focus.* As a busy woman, you're pulled in every direction. But have you evaluated your busyness recently? For instance, are you sufficiently involved in the really important areas of life? Are you possibly wasting time running around being busy with secondary efforts and having little time for the primary areas of family, home, and ministry? Paul wrote in Philippians 3:13, "But *one* thing I do." Make sure you're not living by "these many things I dabble in." Goals are wonderful because they put boundaries on your life. They bring calm in the midst of chaos. Having goals ensures that you concentrate on the most important events and decline the others. Focus gives a sense of contentment as you move forward and accomplish specific steps day by day.

*Goals provide motivation.* I am so excited every morning when I get out of bed because I know the direction of God's will as defined by my goals. I wrote them based on His Word. I committed them to Him. And I pray through them each day in case He wants me to change them. So I don't have to be anxious about the major direction of my day or where to spend my limited time and energy. I have plans based on goals forged with God's help. Such a powerful force can be yours too as you establish direction based on what you believe to be the will of God. Then all day long you can allow the enabling power of the Holy Spirit to work through you and your plan as you serve God and others.

*Goals provide guidance.* How do you make decisions? I've found that without goals, my choices are likely to be heavily influenced by the whims and demands of others or made by default. Many decisions on a daily basis are made for the good and well-being of our families, and some are made with some degree of spontaneity. But quite a few could be made because you couldn't think of a good reason to say no. However with goals—goals based on God's will for your life—you'll have a much better idea of how to make the best decisions—godly decisions—that will result in confident and contented and productive living.

### *Five More Reasons Why You Can Be Content*

Are you grasping why goals are important? Goals have been such an anchor in my life that I'm enjoying the reminder of how good they are. I can live in contentment knowing God has given me a map for serving Him via the goals I wrote down many years ago. Sure, they've changed and been modified as life happened, but I've followed God's leading through those goals for the past 25 years... maybe even more. And, Lord willing, I plan to continue to follow their direction until I see Jesus face-to-face and hopefully hear His commendation, "Well done, good and faithful servant, [Elizabeth]!" (Matthew 25:21). Contentment is a wonderful state to be in!

So let's do a little review on why we can be content.

*Reason #1—God is your sun.* You have His provision. Just as the sun is the source of all physical life, so God is the source of all life, both physical and spiritual. *You don't have to worry about provisions.*

*Reason #2—God is your shield.* You have His protection. Just as a shield is protection in war, so God is your source of safety and security. *You don't have to worry about fighting enemies alone.*

*Reason #3—God gives you His grace.* You have His grace, His sufficiency. When you need Him, He provides all things through His grace. *You don't have to worry about being strong enough.*

*Reason #4—God will give you glory.* You have God's promise that He will give you

> glory—eternal glory—no matter how or when you die. *You don't have to worry about your eternal destiny*. And you will experience some of Jesus' glory here on earth!

These are some fantastic reasons why you can trust God and be content, aren't they? But now for the psalmist's fifth and final reason, as listed in Psalm 84:11.

*Reason #5—God gives what is good.*

> For the LORD God is a sun and shield;
> the LORD will give grace and glory;
> no good thing will He withhold
> from those who walk uprightly.

You can be content knowing that your good God only gives what is 100-percent good or beneficial for you. I'm always amazed when I read Jesus' contrast between earthly "evil" fathers who give good gifts to their children and our heavenly Father who does even more for His children:

> What man is there among you who, if his son asks for bread, will give him a stone? Or if he asks for a fish, will he give him a serpent? If you then, being evil, know how to give good gifts to your children, how much more will your Father who is in heaven give good things to those who ask Him! (Matthew 7:9-12).

Living in an affluent society tends to distort our view of what is good. We mistake the "good things" of life in our opinion with what God considers to be "good" in its beneficial effect. Our "good" is often defined by possessions, cars, houses, vacations, and money, the "stuff" of life. But God's "good" is defined by His nature: "Every good gift and every perfect gift is from above, and comes down from the Father of lights" (James 1:17). God's good is perfect, where as our good—mankind's good—is marred by worldly desire, greed, and fluctuating values. God wants to give us that which is *always* good. We need to make sure our "good" lines up with His "good," as revealed in the Bible.

*There are many good things in the world, but you and I need to ask, "Are they the best things for me?"*

Let's explore the truth of God's goodness in Psalm 84:11. First, this is a marvelous fact about God and His nature. Goodness is one of His attributes. And it's also a promise. What have you got? What do you possess? Whatever it is (or isn't!), God has given you the beneficial things that are blessings from above, things you need for your service and pilgramage through life. This includes the necessities of life and may even include some material goods.

But here's a catch: There are many good things in this world, but you and I need to keep asking, "Are these the best things for me?" Here's a simple test from Scripture that will help you decide if something you want or something you want to do is "good," as defined by God's Word, which, of course, means it's something God wants for you.

*Test #1—Is it worthy of a child of God?* "All things are lawful for me, but all things are not helpful..." (1 Corinthians 6:12).

*Test #2—Will it enslave?* "All things are lawful for me, but I will not be brought under the power of any" (1 Corinthians 6:12).

*Test #3—Will it hinder the spiritual growth of others?* "Therefore, if food makes my brother stumble,

I will never again eat meat, lest I make my brother stumble" (1 Corinthians 8:13).

*Test #4— Will it produce spiritual growth?* "All things are lawful for me, but not all things edify" (1 Corinthians 10:23).

To sum up: If you don't have something, you shouldn't want it because it's not what you need or God would have given it to you already. Go ahead and pray, but remember God doesn't withhold anything that is good when it is what's needed right now. So be careful when you *think* you're lacking something and when you set your goals. It's an affront to God and a slur on His character to believe you need something and He isn't supplying it. God's goodness is so utterly and amazingly wonderful!

### *A Contentment Breakthrough*

The concept of trusting God came home to me loud and clear some years ago when, as I shared earlier, Jim left his well-paying job to enroll in seminary. Although I was generally content to live in a smaller house on a lot less money, there were two things I struggled with. They really weren't big things, but they hounded me. Every time I was in our small living room, I had to sit on a sofa with stuffing coming out of its threadbare covering. And when I looked up I was confronted with ugly stains on the ceiling that indicated the roof leaked. Jim's small income was enough to live on but not to replace a couch or fix the roof. Every day I sat on that lumpy couch to pray and looked up at the ceiling with its brown spots. *We have given up so much to serve You, God,* I thought. *Why, oh why, won't You provide help in these two areas?* (I can't believe how bratty I was being.)

After memorizing and meditating on Psalm 84:11, I finally realized God had already given me what was good—and that it was against His nature not to! Since God hadn't seen fit to replace either eyesore, I concluded that I didn't need what He obviously hadn't provided. So I altered my thinking and brought my desires under control, paring them down to meet what my gracious God had already given me. I was finally content!

When I share these insights with women at conferences, I always like to finish with what happened to that roof. Jim and I hosted a Bible study in our little house that met every Friday night. Everyone could clearly see the brown spots on the ceiling. It was impossible not to. And people continually commented on it. I even noticed they positioned their chairs so they wouldn't be under the sagging ceiling…just in case. One Saturday morning our phone rang. Jim answered, but no one was on the line. Then the doorbell rang. Jim went to the door…but no one was there. On the doormat was an envelope full of cash—enough money to fix the roof! We don't know who God used to provide His blessing to us, but we were reminded once again that the good things of God always come according to His timetable. He promises, "No good thing will [I] withhold from those who walk uprightly." And He means it!

## *Sources of Contentment*

Every river has a source. And so it is with God's blessings. As an often-sung doxology expresses, "Praise God from whom all blessings flow." One of God's bountiful blessings that we need so very much is contentment…the contentment only He can give. Look at, acknowledge, and appreciate these sources of precious peace and joy.

*Contentment has its foundation in God.* This can be seen in the five reasons for contentment we've been considering, along with many more that God offers to His children. A lack of contentment means a lack of trust in the provision of God. If I believe that my loving and perfect God will not withhold that which is good and necessary, I have the calm assurance that God will *always* provide. It's that simple! I just need to be patient…and content.

*Contentment comes with focused devotion.* Jesus said people can't serve two masters (Matthew 6:24). Materialism, and especially money and what it buys, can become a master. It's a constant temptation. Money itself isn't bad because it's neutral. It is neither good nor bad. It's "the *love* of money" that becomes our master (1 Timothy 6:10). A true test of your focus is to ask, What person or thing occupies the majority of my thoughts, time, and energy? If your answer isn't God, you're serving the wrong master.

*Contentment is a learned perspective*—Some of the most encouraging verses in the Bible (at least to my heart) are Paul's declaration in Philippians 4:11-12: "I have *learned* in whatever state I am, to be content: I know to be abased, and I know how to abound. Everywhere and in all things I have *learned* both to be full and to be hungry, both to abound and to suffer need."

As you turn more and more of your fears and desires over to God and trust Him and believe in His goodness, you will see how He is faithful to respond to your every real need. And you will trust Him more and more. You, like Paul, will *learn* to be content because you have chosen to trust in your loving, gracious heavenly Father.

## *Moving Forward*

When my girls were young we would often go to the mall to do a little shopping. As soon as we hit the first store, the girls would start their little recording saying, "I want that!" or "Can I have that?" This would go on for as long as we were in the mall. It got pretty irritating after a few stores because they didn't *need* any of what they were wanting. Jim and I, as caring parents, had already given them everything they *needed*...and more.

Too often I'm like that with God! Constantly asking for stuff, and more stuff. How about you? Can you relate? Here's a sobering question: What has God withheld from you that you think you really need? The true answer is "Nothing!" If you needed it, your good

God has already given it to you or will give it to you. Move forward in your journey of following God with all your heart by:

- *acknowledging* God's goodness,
- *thanking* Him for His present provision, and
- *trusting* Him to continue to provide all your needs *as they arise*.

If you do this, you are on the road to becoming a content woman!

*God's promises are like life preservers.*
*They keep the soul from sinking*
*in the sea of trouble.*

20

# Walking in Peace and Freedom

*For the LORD God is a sun and shield;*
*the LORD will give grace and glory;*
*no good thing will He withhold*
*from those who walk uprightly.*

PSALM 84:11

I'm sure you love the welcome given to you by the sun each glorious new day. What a way to wake up, to begin fresh. And to think, God is a sun to you, bringing you energy, joy, hope, and vision.

Here's something else you can count on when you wake up each morning. God promises that "no good thing will He withhold from those who walk uprightly." Whatever is good and good for you, your heavenly Father will give it, supply it, provide it. This is a promise from Him to you!

And what is a promise? The dictionary defines promise as a statement, either oral or written, assuring that one will or will not do something. A promise is a pledge, vow, or oath. I'm sure you've made a few promises in your life. If you're married, you exchanged wedding vows and pledged your undying love to your husband. If you're a member of a local church, chances are you agreed to a set of bylaws that regulate the ministry of that church. And as a citizen, you pledge your allegiance to the flag and the governmental authorities of the nation. You have quite a bit of experience with promises, vows, and pledges.

### *Learning About God's Promises*

In this section we've been searching for the road that leads to contentment. And we've discovered five provisions—five promises!—from God to us in Psalm 84:11:

- God is a sun.
- God is a shield.
- God gives grace.
- God gives glory.
- God is good and gives good gifts.

And what allows us to know that He will follow through? That we can depend on these promises? The answer is found in the very nature of God. *The power of any promise depends on the one making the promise.* This means you can trust in God's promises of provision, protection, peace, ultimate glory, and goodness because of His character, His attributes. God is the God "who cannot lie" (Titus 1:2). This is who God is! You can accept with assurance any promise He makes in His Word, including the ones in Psalm 84. And good news! There are a *lot* of other wonderful promises to you in the Bible! Some scholars estimate there are as many as 8,000!

God genuinely and perfectly loves and cares for His creation—including you. His lovingkindness has been proven by His many promises and their fulfillment through the ages. But there are a few facts about God's promises to keep in mind:

- Many promises are limited to *specific* people or groups of people, such as Abraham and God's promise of the land of Israel; Jacob's family and

God's promise that they would return from exile; King David and God's promise to him of an eternal kingdom.

- Many promises are *unlimited* and apply to believers for all time.
- Many of God's promises are *conditional.* This means God will do something or give something, but you are to do something in return or give something as well.

### *Receiving God's Promises*

In Psalm 84:11 God promises to be our sun and shield and to give grace, glory, and all the good things we will ever need. However, He has one condition:

> No good thing will He withhold
> from those who walk uprightly.

Think about it. Experiencing the full impact and benefit of these promises hinges on the condition that *you walk uprightly.* As several other versions translate it:

- "To innocent lives, He will never refuse His bounty."
- "He does not withhold prosperity from those who live blamelessly."[1]

God is a limitless giver. He *loves* to give, and He *wants* to give. It's His nature to give. But when it comes to His promises in Psalm 84:11, if we refuse to obey God's one condition, we will suffer and fail to receive and enjoy the blessings He offers that lead to contentment, peace, and freedom. All He asks is that we walk uprightly, that we live an innocent and blameless life. Our disobedience limits our ability to receive God's giving. Our lack of trust in God limits our blessings. Although I don't know who wrote this, the wisdom and truth is life-changing!

> God makes a promise—
> Faith believes it,
> Hope anticipates it,
> Patience quietly awaits it,
> Love notes any condition and obeys it.

Love obeys God's commands and conditions. To receive the blessings God gives in Psalm 84, verse 11, we must walk uprightly and blamelessly.

### *Living Blamelessly*

Living blamelessly? Is this even possible? No, it isn't...if we're talking sinless perfection. No one was or is without sin, except Jesus. So being blameless or walking uprightly must mean something else. To walk uprightly *is* to follow God with all your heart. It's your deep desire to walk with Him so closely that your conduct is more and more godly, more and more like Him, more and more Christlike. It's seeking to be blameless in your heart and in your actions. The very fact that God promises to honor this kind of person means that walking uprightly is possible. You say, "No, it can't be done!" But that's not true. God never asks us to do something without giving us the means. Read on!

Once upon a time there was a godly couple—a couple after God's own heart. They both loved God and sought with all their hearts to walk in all His ways. And yet they suffered the heartache of having no children, a serious social and religious stigma in their culture. Their life was less than ideal, and not what they had dreamed it would be. Yet here is God's forever description of Elizabeth and her husband, Zacharias:

> And they were both righteous before God, walking in all the commandments and ordinances of the Lord blameless (Luke 1:6).

And here's another example—Maria Taylor, the wife of Hudson Taylor, missionary to China and founder of China Inland Mission. On her deathbed, Mrs. Taylor said to her husband, "You know, darling, that for ten years past there has not been a cloud between me and my Savior. I cannot be sorry to go to Him." For 10 years not a cloud between her and God. Now *that* is living an upright life! A life where there is no resentment, no bitterness, no grudges between you and God. This also signifies a life where there was no resentment, grudges, or bitterness toward another person. Blameless in heart!

Like Elizabeth, Zacharias, and Maria Taylor, you can enjoy the blessings of God's promises (including those listed in Psalm 84:11)! What do you need to do?

## *Watch Out for Sin*

*Sin*—falling short of God's standards as revealed in His Word—limits your life. It keeps you from partaking of the many blessings God wants to shower upon you. It also impedes your ability to serve the Lord and others. Every day you have a choice about how you will live your life. God says, "Don't sin! Choose to walk uprightly and be blessed and be a blessing to others." This means: Watch out for sin and deal with it when it comes along.

Satan and his world system says just the opposite: "Live as you like. Do your own thing. Do what you want to do. If it feels good, do it. Live with no restraints, no rules, no limitations. That's real freedom!" But according to God, those who practice the world's definition of freedom will miss out on the ultimate freedom and provision, protection, grace, glory, and good He offers. That's a heavy price to pay for do-your-own-thing, feel-good moments!

As one who doesn't want to miss out on any of God's blessings, my thinking goes like this: I must deal with sin—any sin, all sin, every sin, large sins, and small sins—because every sin is still sin in God's eyes. That's why I try to follow these steps for following God with all my heart.

- *Search for sin.* Ask God in prayer, "Search me, O God, and know my heart...see if there is any wicked way in me" (Psalm 139:23-24).
- *Acknowledge sin.* Once sin is discovered, name it, acknowledge it, and own it. Don't deny it, tuck it away, rationalize it, or gloss over it. And don't blame others for it. "For every sin, Satan is ready to provide an excuse." Do as David did when he poured out his heart to God: "I acknowledged my sin to You, and my iniquity I have not hidden" (Psalm 32:5).
- *Confess sin.* Confession is simply admitting a wrong. Confess your sin to your holy, all-knowing God. David's prayer continues, "I will confess my transgressions to the LORD" (verse 5).
- *Receive forgiveness.* The greatest benefit from confession is the freedom and relief it brings. David continues his outpouring: "And You forgave the iniquity of my sin" (verse 5). And the blessed result? David writes in verse 1: "Blessed [or happy] is he whose transgression is forgiven, whose sin is covered."
- *Move on!* With the debilitating guilt of his sin removed and the freedom of forgiveness in his heart, David was right back on track with God. He was walking with God and basking in His bountiful blessings. He was once again free to live God's plan and serve God and His people. David quotes God in verse 8, "I will instruct you and teach you in the way you should go."

### *Confronting Sin in Real Life*

I've shared in several of my books about the time I lived under the shadow of the possibility that Jim would be deployed to the Middle East during Operation Desert Storm. How did I manage this crisis in my life?

I chose to pray and fast every day until the evening meal for as long as the potential of Jim's military call-up existed. But fasting and prayers wouldn't mean anything if I didn't deal with sin. So my first step each day and with each prayer was to ask, "God, is there anything in my life that might keep You from answering my prayers for my husband and family?" And when God brought anything to my attention, I made every effort to take care of it and deal with it before God and in my life.

For instance, one thing God brought to my mind was our financial giving at church. We were giving, but not on a regular basis. It was more like whenever we remembered or got around to it. We were not being faithful in obedience in this area of our Christian lives (1 Corinthians 16:2; 2 Corinthians 9:6-8). I didn't want to neglect anything God asked of me as I prayed for Jim's continued presence at home. When I shared my conviction about giving with Jim, we quickly acknowledged and confessed this failure to God and began to be more faithful. We weren't trying to buy God's favor. We were responding to His teaching in the Bible regarding an area of faithful obedience.

### *Practicing Your Priorities*

Another way to walk uprightly is to practice your God-given priorities. Keeping a clean slate with God concerning sin keeps the channel of fellowship open with Him. Practicing your priorities keeps you open to living out God's will. Just as God's Word tells you about sin and how to deal with it, so His Word reveals your roles and responsibilities. His priorities for women involve:

- *Walking with the Lord*—to grow spiritually through reading and studying Scripture and through mentoring.
- *Family*—to foster a deep commitment to love, serve, support, and pray faithfully for family members.
- *Home*—to create a nurturing atmosphere and a place of beauty and order for others.
- *Ministry*—to give and grow in service and encouragement to others.

You walk uprightly when you pursue God's priorities for your life. This really gets down to the basics of life. For instance, I talked to a woman recently who told me she hadn't spoken to her husband for 16 days. Friend, that's 16 days of not walking uprightly! That's 16 days without God's blessings! That's 16 days of unanswered prayer! Her silence was willful, and it was daily. Her husband had done something she didn't like, so she punished him by giving him the cold shoulder. Choosing to disobey God's design for honoring one another in marriage is sin.

Another example occurred when a mom called me with a frazzled plea for help. "Everything is in shambles and falling apart. I'm at my wit's end!" Once I helped her calm down, I asked, "What should you be doing that you're not doing?" There was a deafening pause. "Well," she sheepishly began, "I'm not getting up in the morning. So my family is on their own. I can't seem to get around to the laundry, so we don't have any clean clothes. I'm so tired in the evening that I have my husband pick up takeout on the way home from work. Everything is in chaos!"

*Peace and love and joy will reign in your heart and home when you pursue God's will.*

Does it sound like God is blessing this woman's life? Do you think her family is reaping the consequences of her neglect, her laziness? And what does Proverbs 31:27 say? "She watches over the ways of her household, and does not eat the bread of idleness." That's God's will. That's God's plan. That's God's priority. Yes, every woman has a frazzled day here and there, but that's not to be the norm.

Peace and love and joy can reign in a woman's heart *and* home when she pursues God's will in her home. The result? "Her children rise up and call her blessed; her husband also, and he praises her" (Proverbs 31:28).

So, dear reader, your roles are clearly defined—spiritual growth, love and care for family, service to God and others. If you want God's blessings in your life, you must seek with all your heart to walk uprightly as you practice the priorities God designed for you!

## *Moving Forward*

Have you been counting your blessings? Psalm 84:11 is loaded with them. Blessings that span every facet, age, stage, and need of your life. And all of them add up to contentment...sweet contentment. In one verse out of the 31,000-plus verses in the Bible, God gives you *five* provisions with only one condition. He offers you *five* promises and only asks *one* thing of you. To continue to move forward in following God with all your heart, there's only one thing you must do—walk uprightly. God is your sun and shield. God gives you grace and glory. God withholds no good thing. All of these blessings are yours when you do your part—love God enough to keep His commandments (John 14:15).

My precious reading friend, you *can* be content because you have everything God intends you to have for this very moment. And when you step into the next moment, you'll have everything then too. When you pare your desires down to what you have, realizing you have everything God wants to give you for your present needs and well being, you will be content. You will be satisfied.

You will be in agreement with God about His goodness and provision. Trust Him for today and for your glorious end. Every place you stop along the way as you travel with Him, walking uprightly, your soul will be at rest.

Charles H. Spurgeon, renowned British preacher and pastor, often quoted the last two stanzas of an old German choral music composition that revealed the deep contentment found in Psalm 84:

> Own Thou the Lord to be thy sun, thy shield—
> No good will He withhold;
> He giveth grace, and soon shall be revealed
> His glory, yet untold.
>
> His mighty name confessing,
> Walk thou at peace, and free;
> O Lord, how rich the blessing
> Of him who trusts in Thee!

Section 6

# *Becoming a Confident Woman*

*To serve the present age,*

*my calling to fulfill;*

*O may it all my powers engage*

*to do my Master's will!*[1]

CHARLES WESLEY

# 21

# *Believing and Living God's Plan*

*I can do all things through*
*Christ who strengthens me.*

PHILIPPIANS 4:13

If you came to my house and walked into our library, you would immediately surmise that Jim and I are students of the Bible. Because we're both Bible teachers, we have shelves of Bible commentaries, Bible dictionaries, and Bible encyclopedias, along with numerous devotional works and volumes on theology and Christian living. But what might surprise you is that we also have a few books from the "Chicken Soup" series.[2] These books contain wonderful and instructive stories about real-life people. I've especially identified with the volume *Chicken Soup for the Writer's Soul* for obvious reasons.

One story from a Chicken Soup book that was moving and inspiring was about a young Girl Scout whose mom had always wished to go on a trip with her daughter. However, being a single mom working as a waitress, the mother and daughter hardly had enough money for the basics, let alone for travel.

This teen girl noticed in her Girl Scout magazine that the scout member who sold the most cookies during the upcoming year would win an all-expense-paid trip around the world for herself and a parent. This 13-year-old girl wasn't any smarter than the other scouts, nor was she more outgoing. In fact, she was extremely shy. But she had a dream for her mom and believed she could sell many boxes of cookies.

The outcome? When the cookie-selling season was over and the final figures were in, she'd sold 3,526 boxes of cookies. She won the trip around the world for her and her mom! Since then Markita Andrews has sold more than 42,000 boxes of cookies and is regularly asked to speak at sales and motivational seminars for corporations around the world![3]

This girl believed something and confidently went about making it happen. But as inspiring as her story is, you and I have the opportunity to achieve even greater results in our lives.

### *Taking a Walk*

Maybe you and I won't sell 40,000-plus (or even 40!) boxes of cookies, but as we trust God and believe in His plan for us, we too can achieve great and amazing things and live lives of maximum usefulness to God. How is this possible? For me it started with aiming at a daily goal of taking a walk.

Some months into this new discipline, I found I needed something to do with my *mind* on my walks! So I began carrying a packet of Bible verses to memorize and think about. On one particular morning—a life-changing morning!—I picked up a fresh batch of verses as I headed out the door. My first verse was Philippians 4:13:

> I can do all things through Christ
> who strengthens me.

My friend, even as a writer I'll never find the words to express the impact these ten words had on my life that day...and every day since. I had to stop right there on the sidewalk as the truth and power of this single verse hit me. I had stumbled upon the ultimate confidence builder! I repeated the astounding, incredible words again and again.

To this day when I'm walking outside or on my treadmill, if whatever is going on in my life causes me to worry or fret (I tend to be a bit of a worrywart), out comes this verse now stored in my heart. I've leaned on this verse while caring for my aging parents and their needs. I turn to it when my ever-present, ever-full, ever-pressing schedule gets cumbersome. At the time I discovered the power of this verse, I had two college-age daughters with their schooling, dating lives, and their concerns about the future accompanying me on my walks. And always there are Jim's and my list of deadlines, commitments, and pressures. Plus there are the normal slate of heartaches that come with interpersonal relationships—gossip, slander, misunderstanding, criticism. And don't forget physical problems that pop up occasionally.

Yes, these and several hundred more cares tag along with me uninvited on my walks. But so does Philippians 4:13! And out it comes as each worry springs up like an unwelcome weed. There the truth is—the dazzling promise and stabilizing power of God's promise. It's right there with me—in me—at all times. It never fails to encourage my soul and strengthen me for what's in front of me as I follow God. And it bolsters my confidence as I deal with the issues of living out God's plan. I'm still awed that I can do all things—and learning what "all things" encompasses!—through Christ who strengthens me.

## *Understanding True Confidence*

The world's idea of "confidence" is based on self-reliance—personal abilities and resources that can make things happen. But the confidence spoken of in Philippians 4:13 is *God*-reliance. Sense this truth as you consider these translations of verse 13:

- "I have strength for all things in him which giveth me power."
- "Nothing is beyond my power in the strength of him who makes me strong."

- "I am ready for anything through the strength of the one who lives within me."
- "I can do everything God asks me to with the help of Christ who gives me the strength and power."[4]

Where did this glorious verse come from? Answer: Inspired by God and written by the apostle Paul. While in prison, Paul wrote this letter to encourage and strengthen his Christian friends in Philippi. The theme of the book of Philippians is life in Christ.

In chapter 4, Paul especially points to the presence of Christ in every life situation. After listing a few specific challenges of his own (being abased, suffering need, going hungry, even the extreme of having too much), Paul basically concludes, "Not only can I endure and deal with these kinds of things, but I can do so in *all* things!" How? Through Christ, who infused him with His power for any situation, at any time, and for however long.

*Through Christ you gain strength to do, accomplish, and endure anything.*

Paul isn't talking about self-sufficiency. Oh no! He's letting the whole world know his sufficiency lay in a Person other than himself, the Person who promised and followed through by empowering him to do all things—anything it took—to follow God with all his heart. Picture being hooked up to an IV to receive life-sustaining fluids and nutrients. In the same way, Christ infuses and fills you with His strength and His power. Through Christ you gain the strength you need to do, accomplish, and endure anything. Christ's power is a sure confidence builder.

### *Increasing Your Confidence*

Think about your life and your worries and challenges. What is your greatest fear? Your heaviest dread? Name it...and then lay the truth of Philippians 4:13 next to it. God's Word is telling you that in all things—in each thing, every thing, any thing, in every condition separately or all these conditions together—there is nothing you can't do, accomplish, overcome, triumph in. There is nothing you can't bear, suffer, or endure! Why? Because Christ strengthens you! Put this scripture to work for you.

✓ Paul could face anything...and so can you.

✓ Paul had Christ in every situation...and so do you.

✓ Paul looked to Christ as his help, his fountain of wisdom...and so can you.

✓ Paul received encouragement, energy, and confidence for his every need through this assurance...and so can you.

The woman who walks with Christ can successfully cope with anything and everything. Now, *that* is true confidence based on God's truth!

### *Following God with All Your Heart*

When I think of Philippians 4:13 and God's provision for complete confidence, I see it as God's end-all verse. When we put our faith in God into action and take the steps—and the risks—involved in following Him with all our hearts, we can do "all things"! This verse is God's exclamation point for all His promises. Now, with the truth of Philippians 4:13 in mind, let's review the scriptures and promises we've discovered.

*God's promise of success.* Success God's way! You are following God with all your heart when you know His Word...and obey it. And you will enjoy His success and blessings along the way! "This Book of the Law shall not depart from your mouth, but you shall meditate in it day and night, that you may observe to do according to all that is written in it. For then you will make your way prosperous, and then you will have good success" (Joshua 1:8).

*God's promise of courage.* Courage for following God with all your heart comes when you count on His presence. "Have I not commanded you? Be strong and of good courage; do not be afraid, nor be dismayed, for the LORD your God is with you wherever you go" (Joshua 1:9).

*God's promise of an exceptional life.* You are following God with all your heart when you think His thoughts and live His will. "Do not be conformed to this world, but be transformed by the renewing of your mind, that you may prove what is that good and acceptable and perfect will of God" (Romans 12:2).

*God's promise of humility.* You are following God with all your heart when you humbly do what is right, trusting Him to choose the time to lift you up and reward you. "All of you be submissive to one another, and be clothed with humility, for 'God resists the proud, but gives grace to the humble.' Therefore humble yourselves under the mighty hand of God, that He may exalt you in due time" (1 Peter 5:5-6).

*God's promise of contentment.* You are following God with all your heart when you believe in His goodness and provision and walk in all His ways. "For the LORD God is a sun and shield; the LORD will give grace and glory; no good thing will He withhold from those who walk uprightly" (Psalm 84:11).

*God's promise of strength.* You are following God with all your heart when you believe in His power and count on it. "I can do all things through Christ who strengthens me" (Philippians 4:13).

## *Moving Forward*

I hope you realize by now that you truly can follow God with all your heart. There will never be an obstacle you cannot navigate around. There will never be a difficulty you cannot manage. There will never be a pain you cannot bear. And there will never be a challenge you cannot overcome. As God's child you can do everything God asks you to do through the strength of Christ who *lives* in you, *gives* you power, and *makes* you strong—strong enough to follow and trust Him completely.

# Notes

## An Invitation

1. Psalm 2:11; John 4:24; Ephesians 2:10.
2. Proverbs 3:6; Deuteronomy 4:29; 13:3; Psalm 86:12; 1 Kings 14:8; Deuteronomy 10:12.

## Chapter 1 — Success Made Simple

1. See the book of Numbers, ch. 1.

## Chapter 3 —The Road to Success

1. Christian educator Kathi Hudson, in Roy B. Zuck, *The Speaker's Quote Book* (Grand Rapids, MI: Kregel Publications, 1997), p. 363.
2. Matthew Henry, *Matthew Henry's Commentary on the Whole Bible* (Peabody, MA: Hendrickson Publishers, 1991), p. 290.

## Chapter 4 —A Sure Recipe for Success

1. Drawn from John C. Maxwell, *Running with the Giants* (New York: Warner Books, 2002), p. 58.

## Chapter 6 — Facing the Impossible

1. Elisabeth Elliot, *Let Me Be a Woman* (Wheaton, IL: Tyndale House, 1977), pp. 75, 97.
2. Herbert Lockyer, *The Women of the Bible* (Grand Rapids, MI: Zondervan Publishing House, 1975), p. 64.
3. Edith Schaeffer, *What Is a Family?* (Old Tappan NJ: Fleming H. Revell Company, 1975), pp. 13-33.

## Chapter 7 — Fighting Your Fears

1. Original source unknown, taken from Frank S. Mead, ed., *12,000 Religious Quotations* (Grand Rapids, MI: Baker Book House, 2000), p. 143.
2. F.B. Meyer, quoted in D.L. Moody, *Notes from My Bible and Thoughts from My Library* (Grand Rapids, MI: Baker Book House, 1979), pp. 43-44.

## Chapter 10 — Making a Difference

1. Bruce B. Barton, David R. Veerman, Neil Wilson, *Life Application Bible Commentary—Romans* (Wheaton, IL: Tyndale House Publishers, Inc., 1992), p. 231.
2. See Ephesians 4:25; James 5:12; Ephesians 4:15.
3. See Colossians 3:8; Ephesians 4:29,31.

## Chapter 11 — Renewing Your Mind

1. D.L. Moody, *Notes from My Bible and Thoughts from My Library* (Grand Rapids, MI: Baker Book House, 1979), p. 258.

## Chapter 12 — Following God's Will

1. Cecil Rhodes, in A. Naismith, *Treasure of Notes, Quotes, Anecdotes* (Grand Rapids, MI: Baker Book House, 1976), p. 253.
2. Elizabeth George, *A Woman After God's Own Heart* (Eugene, OR: Harvest House Publishers, 2006) and Elizabeth George, *A Woman's Call to Prayer* (Eugene, OR: Harvest House Publishers, 2004). For more of my books, see the list in the back of this book.

## Chapter 13 — Laying a Foundation of Humility

1. Charles Caldwell Ryrie, *The Ryrie Study Bible* (Chicago: Moody Press, 1978), p. 1870.
2. See 1 Corinthians 11:3; Ephesians 5:22,24; Colossians 3:18; Titus 2:5.

## Chapter 15 — Seeing Humility in Action

1. M.R. DeHaan and Henry G. Bosch, *Our Daily Bread* (Grand Rapids MI: Zondervan Publishing House, 1982), December 2.
2. See Romans 1:1; Philippians 1:1; Titus 1:1.

### Chapter 16 — Walking the Less-Traveled Road of Humility

1. Matthew 14:29-30; 16:21-22; Luke 22:33.

### Chapter 17 — Looking for Contentment in All the Wrong Places

1. *Common Worship: Services and Prayers for the Church of England* (London: The Archbishops' Council of the Church of England, 2000-2006), "Night Prayer" (Compline), "Collect" option.

### Chapter 18 — Living with Grace and Glory

1. Julia H. Johnston, "Grace Greater Than Our Sin," *Hymns Tried and True* (Chicago: Bible Institute Colportage Association, 1911), #2.

### Chapter 20 — Walking in Peace and Freedom

1. Curtis Vaughan, *The New Testament from 26 Translations* (Grand Rapids, MI: Zondervan Publishing House, 1967).

### Chapter 21 — Believing and Living God's Plan

1. William J. Petersen and Randy Petersen, *One Year Book of Psalms* (Wheaton, IL: Tyndale House Publishers, Inc., 1999), July 6.
2. Jack Canfield and Mark Hansen, et al., *Chicken Soup Series* (Deerfield Beach, FL: Health Communications, Inc.).
3. Jack Canfield and Mark Victor Hansen, *Chicken Soup for the Soul: Living Your Dreams* (Deerfield Beach, FL: Health Communications, Inc., 2003), pp. 238-41.
4. Curtis Vaughan, *The New Testament from 26 Translations* (Grand Rapids, MI: Zondervan Publishing House, 1967), p. 913.


## *About the Author*

**Elizabeth George** is a bestselling author who has more than 4.8 million books in print. She is a popular speaker at Christian women's events. Her passion is to teach the Bible in a way that changes women's lives. For information about Elizabeth's speaking ministry, to sign up for her mailings, or to purchase her books visit her website:

www.ElizabethGeorge.com

## Books by Elizabeth George

- Beautiful in God's Eyes
- Finding God's Path Through Your Trials
- Following God with All Your Heart
- Life Management for Busy Women
- Loving God with All Your Mind
- A Mom After God's Own Heart
- Powerful Promises for Every Woman
- The Remarkable Women of the Bible
- Small Changes for a Better Life
- Walking with the Women of the Bible
- A Wife After God's Own Heart
- A Woman After God's Own Heart®
- A Woman After God's Own Heart® Deluxe Edition
- A Woman After God's Own Heart®—A Daily Devotional
- A Woman After God's Own Heart® Collection
- A Woman's Call to Prayer
- A Woman's High Calling
- A Woman's Walk with God
- A Young Woman After God's Own Heart
- A Young Woman After God's Own Heart—A Devotional
- A Young Woman's Call to Prayer
- A Young Woman's Walk with God

### *Children's Books*

- God's Wisdom for Little Girls
- A Little Girl After God's Own Heart

### *Study Guides*

- Beautiful in God's Eyes Growth & Study Guide
- Finding God's Path Through Your Trials Growth & Study Guide
- Following God with All Your Heart Growth & Study Guide
- Life Management for Busy Women Growth & Study Guide
- Loving God with All Your Mind Growth & Study Guide
- A Mom After God's Own Heart Growth & Study Guide
- The Remarkable Women of the Bible Growth & Study Guide
- Small Changes for a Better Life Growth & Study Guide
- A Wife After God's Own Heart Growth & Study Guide
- A Woman After God's Own Heart® Growth & Study Guide
- A Woman's Call to Prayer Growth & Study Guide
- A Woman's High Calling Growth & Study Guide
- A Woman's Walk with God Growth & Study Guide

### *Books by Jim & Elizabeth George*

- God Loves His Precious Children
- God's Wisdom for Little Boys
- A Little Boy After God's Own Heart

### *Books by Jim George*

- The Bare Bones Bible™ Handbook
- The Bare Bones Bible™ Bios
- A Husband After God's Own Heart
- A Man After God's Own Heart
- The Remarkable Prayers of the Bible
- A Young Man After God's Own Heart